William Waller

Vindication of the Character and Conduct of Sir William Waller

Knight, Commander in Chief of Parliament Forces in the West

William Waller

Vindication of the Character and Conduct of Sir William Waller
Knight, Commander in Chief of Parliament Forces in the West

ISBN/EAN: 9783337279660

Printed in Europe, USA, Canada, Australia, Japan

Cover: Foto ©ninafisch / pixelio.de

More available books at **www.hansebooks.com**

VINDICATION

OF THE

CHARACTER AND CONDUCT

OF

SIR *WILLIAM WALLER,*

KNIGHT;

COMMANDER IN CHIEF OF THE PARLIAMENT
FORCES IN THE WEST:

Explanatory of his Conduct in taking up Arms against
KING CHARLES THE FIRST.

(WRITTEN BY HIMSELF.)
And now First Published from the Original Manuscript.
WITH AN
INTRODUCTION BY THE EDITOR.

Embellished with Portraits of Sir WILLIAM WALLER,

AND OF

J. LENTHALL, ESQ. Speaker of CROMWELL's Parliament.

LONDON:

PRINTED FOR J. DEBRETT, OPPOSITE BURLINGTON-
HOUSE, PICCADILLY.

MDCCXCIII.

INTRODUCTION.

SIR William Waller, as well the author as the subject of the following Vindication, was descended from the ancient family of the Wallers of Speldhurst in the county of Kent, being the son of Sir Thomas Waller, Constable of Dover Castle, and Margaret daughter of Lord and Lady Dacre, and received his first education at Magdalen and Hart Halls in the University of Oxford, which he afterwards compleated at Paris.

He began his military career in the service of the confederate princes against the Emperor,

Emperor, in which he acquired the reputation of a good foldier, and upon his return home was knighted.

He was thrice married, firſt to Jane daughter and heirefs of Sir Richard Reynell of Ford in Devonſhire, by whom he had one daughter Margaret, married to Sir William Courtenay of Powderham Caſtle, anceſtor of the preſent Lord Viſcount Courtenay; ſecondly to the Lady Anne Finch daughter of the firſt Earl of Winchelſea, by whom he had one ſon William, who was afterwards an active magiſtrate for the county of Middleſex, and a ſtrenuous oppoſer of all the meaſures of King Charles the Second's government; and one daughter Anne, married to Sir Philip Harcourt, only ſon of Sir William's third wife Anne, daughter of William Lord Paget, by her firſt huſband Sir Simon Harcourt, from which marriage the preſent Earl of Harcourt is deſcended.

Sir William was elected a member of

the

the Long Parliament for Andover, and having suffered under the severity of the Star-chamber on the occasion of a private quarrel with one of his wife's relations, and imbibed in the course of his foreign service early and warm prejudices in favour of the Presbyterian discipline, he became (as many good men then were) a decided opponent of the court; and having distinguished himself by his first military exploits after the war commenced, was considered as a man prepared to go all lengths that the most furious reformers could propose, and on that account extolled by many as a general to be set in opposition to the Earl of Essex.

While he was yet employed under the Earl of Essex, he was deputed to the command of the important expedition against Portsmouth, when Colonel Goring returning to his duty declared he was resolved to hold that garrison for his Majesty. In this exploit he conducted himself with an ability and diligence that would have done honour to any cause, and having reduced the garrison in a shorter time and upon better terms than could possibly have been expected, his success procured him the conduct of several other expeditions, in all of which, by the great celerity with which he performed his marches, and by his uniform success, he acquired the brilliant title of William the Conqueror.

In the pursuit of the war the character of Sir William Waller never deviated from that gallant courtesy which distinguished the gentlemen of that age, and has ever been the characteristick of an English officer. A letter from him to Sir Ralph Hopton, afterwards Lord Hopton, before the battle of Lansdown, has been preserved, and deserves to be recorded in this publication.

Page 13.

The detail of Sir William Waller's military conduct belongs to the general history of that interesting period. After many

many fignal advantages he fuftained fome defeats by the King's forces, particularly at Roundway Down near the Devizes, and at Cropready-bridge in Oxfordfhire. The blame on each occafion was thrown by him on the jealoufy of other officers, and neither the fpirit nor the judgment of his own operations were ever queftioned. The independents, who were becoming the ftrongeft party in the army and in the Parliament, had wifhed to make him their general, on terms which from confcience or military honour he could not comply with. By the famous felf-denying ordinance he was laid afide as a commander, but ftill preferved fo great an influence and reputation in the army, as made him very formidable to the rifing party. He was confidered as a leader of the Prefbyterians againft the defigns of the independents.—The ftruggle between thefe two parties after the king had fallen into their power is defcribed more particularly in the

the work now published, than in any other memorial of that time; and on that account alone, it forms a valuable addition to the collection of pieces relative to the History of England at that interesting period. He became particularly obnoxious to the leaders of that army which he had in vain attempted to bring into a submission to the orders of the Parliament, which had raised a force for its own destruction, and was one of the eleven members impeached by that army of high treason. Upon this he was forced to withdraw for some time, but that storm at length subsiding he returned to his seat in the House of Commons, till he was with fifty others expelled by the army, and was afterwards committed to different prisons on suspicion of being, with many other Presbyterians, attached to his lawful sovereign, and repenting him of his betrayed allegiance.

He was, indeed, at length sensible of the misery which he had contributed to bring on on his country; he was convinced by fatal experience, that anarchy was a bad ſtep towards a perfect Government—that the ſubverſion of every eſtabliſhment was no ſafe foundation for a permanent and regular Conſtitution; he found that pretences of reform were held up by the deſigning to dazzle the eyes of the unwary, and lead them on to engage in meaſures without knowing either what thoſe meaſures were, or by what means they were to be compaſſed—he found, in ſhort, that reformation, by popular inſurrection, muſt end in the deſtruction, and cannot tend to the formation of a regular Government.

He had, at laſt, the happineſs of living to ſee the monarchy again reſtored, and the Conſtitution ſettled upon its ancient and true principles; but before that event happened, he had, at his leiſure, compoſed the following Vindication of his conduct during thoſe unhappy times; which Vindication hath hitherto been but little known,

known, and is now published from the manuscript in the possession of one of the noble families descended from him.

The reflection upon those scenes in which Sir William Waller had himself performed so considerable a part, will (it is presumed) be found not inapplicable in many parts, to the circumstances of the present day.

It must, however, be constantly kept in mind, at what period the work was written; and those things which are suitable only to that period must not be objected against as irrelevant to the present.

When faction hath once overstepped the boundaries of allegiance, the same arguments which might in the first instance have stopped its career, will not be sufficient to induce it to return. Every argument, therefore, which ingenuity can devise, may and ought to be used upon such an occasion. Logick may be assisted by sophistry, and splendid fallacies may be called in to the support of plain truth.

Points upon which the mind has been already misled, must be those upon which stress must be laid to bring the same mind back into the right way; when the object of persuasion is just, no arguments by which any one may be convinced, ought to be neglected; and when reference is had to the same work upon a second occasion, it is not to be expected that those grounds, which originally might have operated most strongly to persuasion, are to be held in the same estimation upon the second production.

The history of monarchical authority, therefore, as deduced from divine origin, upon which Sir William Waller lays so much stress, might have had great effect at a time when enthusiasm and hypocrisy were prevalent upon every occasion. In these days, however, such topicks of argument would in all probability have but little weight with the multitude; and as to those who are capable of understanding the just principles of civil authority, they know

that

that it is a certain truth, that the power which is not of GOD, cannot stand long, that Government itself is of divine institution, according to the principles of social order implanted in the mind of man by the Almighty Creator and Preserver of Mankind; and that although no peculiar modification of Government is of positive divine institution, yet, that which hath long prevailed in any country, cannot be overturned without the danger of destroying all those relations and interests, which Government is formed to protect and secure.

This part of the work, therefore, might perhaps have been omitted in the publication without any inconvenience, and would probably have been but little regretted; but it was thought improper to mutilate or alter the work in any respect, but that it ought to be given to the publick exactly as the author himself left it, with all its merits and imperfections.

The

The general reflections which the thinking reader ought to draw from this Vindication, are such only as every man must suggest to himself, who knows the event of those unhappy times, and the measures which have but too successfully been pursued in another country, and are now attempted to be practised in this.

Of those men who are engaged in the present attempts to excite sedition, the leaders possessed of talents adequate to their designs, and of reputation great enough to impose upon the unwary by the semblance of publick virtue, may reflect (if men who sacrifice character and honour to the ambition of being leaders in such a business can reflect), that those who first scatter the seeds of sedition are unequal to the gathering in of the harvest; that the multitude is an engine easily to be set in motion, but when checked, that it recoils with an encreased force upon its mover—that it is easy to break down the mounds

of

of the ocean, and to say, " Thus far shall thou go, and no further," but that to stop the tide is given to no presumptuous man; Omnipotence hath reserved to itself alone the power to compose the storm and make the waves subside.

The deluded followers may perceive, that those who pretend to take the part of the people, wish only to be themselves the tyrants—that GOD has fixed the station of men in different degrees, that to attempt to correct the nature of mankind is to war with providence. And both leaders and followers may together reflect, that upon speculative and visionary reformers, the severest punishment which GOD in his vengeance ever yet inflicted, was to curse them with the compleat gratification of their own inordinate desires.

Copy of a Letter from Sir WILLIAM WALLER to Sir RALPH HOPTON, afterwards Lord HOPTON, 1643.

SIR,

THE experience which I have had of your worth, and the happinesse which I have enjoyed in your friendship, are wounding considerations to me, when I look upon this present distance between us: certainly, Sir, my affections to you are so unchangeable, that hostilitie itself cannot violate my friendship to your person; but I must be true to the cause wherein I serve. The old limitation of usque ad aras *holdeth still*; and where my conscience is interested, all other obligations are swallowed up. I should wait on you according to your desire, but that I look on you as ingaged in that partie beyond the possibilitie of retreat, and consequentlie incapable of being wrought upon by anti-persuasion, and I know the conference could never be so close betwixt us, but that it would take wind and receive a construction to my dishonour. That Great God,

God, *who is the searcher of all hearts knows, what a sad fear I go upon this service, and with what a perfect hate I detest a war without an enemie, but I look upon it as* opus Domini, *which is anough to silence all passion in me. The God of Peace send us, in his good time, the blessing of peace, and in the mean time, fit us to receive it. We are both on the stage and must act those parts that are assigned to us in this Tragedy, but let us do it in the way of honour, and without personal animositie; whatsoever the issue of it be, I shall never resigne that dear title, of*

        Your most
           Affectionate Friend .
             and faithful Servant,
                WILLIAM WALLER.

ERRATA.

Page 5. *line* 6. *for* factor *read* factorum.
  9. *line* 17. *for* cecidet *read* cecidit.
  29. *line* 13. *for* carcare *read* cocare.
 148 *line* 6. *for* ridente *read* ridentem.
 189. *line* 18. *for* discendo *read* dicendo.
 246. *line* 23. *for* αβασιλουΐν *read* αβασιλευτοι.
 249. *line* 6. *for* αρχ]αβασιλικ]ο *read* αρχην βασιλικην.
 256. *line* 19. *for* κριμονιαν διδιξωτι *read* ηγιμονιαι διδιξατι.

Directions to the Binder.

Place the Head of Sir WILLIAM WALLER to face the Title page.

The Head of Mr. LENTHALL, to face page 191.

ERRATA.

Page 5, line 6, for Tabor van Tabora,
    — 14, 17, — verslelt read verstelt,
    — 19, line 12, getracht read oreht,
    — 20, — 17, zyn vikande read hiembtm,
    — 24, title, de Literd read Slords,
    — 25, line 1, de hoern makars,
    — 91, — 21, volmedend, read bijzonders,
    — 239, — 9, ycard, haresagers, &c. &c.

Directions to the Binder.

Place the Head of W. William Walter, to face the
    title.

Insert, of Mr. Larrani, to face page 191.

WALLER's VINDICATION,
&c. &c. &c.

IT is true, in common experience, and in the obfervation of all former ages, that innocency could never yet walk alone without a protection, but it became a prey, expofed to falfe arrefts, vexations, and fcandals. Not to fpeak of our Saviour himfelf, traduced for a friend of publicans and finners, a feducer of the people, an enemy to Cæfar: if we look back to antiquity, we may trace the beft of men from time to time, even from the Patriarchs to the Apoftles, and fo downward, and mark the way they have gone, by good report, and bad report; fome perfecuted with bitter mockings,

Luke vii. 34. John, vii. 12. and xix. 12.

mockings, others derided as fools, impeached as seditious persons, conspirators, revolters, rebels; accounted and vilified, as the filth of the world, the offscouring of all things. What shall I say of the primitive Christians, charged with idolatry, impiety, obscenity! insomuch that Quadratus, Aristides, Justine Martyr, Apollinaris, Tertullian, and others, had work enough to apologise for them. These things are written for our example and admonition, who live, in *fæce Romuli,* in the lees and dregs of time, upon whom the ends of the world are come, that we through patience might have hope. And though the consideration of parallels in calamity may seem to be but a kind of ill-natured comfort; yet I suppose it may be justifiable in this sound conclusion; that if those holy men of old have been, by a divine permission, exposed to such malicious prosecutions, notwithstanding their integrity and innocency, I have the less occasion to be dejected with

the

Marginal references: Gen. xxi. 9. Gal. iv. 29. 2 Sam. vi. 20. 1 Kings, xviii. 7. Amos, vii. 10. Jerem. xxxvii. 13. Nehem. vi. 6. 1 Cor. iv. 13. 1 Cor. x. 11. Rom. xv. 4.

the sense of my sufferings, since no new thing is happened unto me; or to think much, after these examples, to be made myself an example.

But Christianity doth not make a man a stock, impassible, insensible: I cannot but feel that pressure that lies upon me; and if I groan under it, I do no more than many of those blessed men did, in the like condition, who had better shoulders than I. It is true, in some cases, it may be interpreted a weakness and folly to complain, as when the case is slight or irremediable; and if there were no more in this business than a mere popular groundless clamour, I should with a quiet scorn have passed it by, and reckoned my silence, not only as a part of speech, as Apollonius did, but as the fittest and best language that I could use; as *aliquid eloquentiæ*, as Cicero phraseth it, to his friend Atticus. Or if again there were so much in it, as would carry the weight of an unanswerable

[side note: Philostrat. in Vit. Apollon. lib. viii. 1. c.]

[side note: Cicero ad Attic.]

able charge, I should have had so much discretion as to lay my hand upon my mouth; and according to Syracides his advice, be as one that knoweth, and yet holdeth his tongue. But when my name and reputation are under an injurious question, prosecuted by a malice masked with the justice of a Parliament, and backed with the power of an army, it were not only a stupidity in me, not to be sensible of it, but my silence might rationally be thought to speak my guiltiness. I confess, I had need be perfect in Pambo's lesson, *Dixi custodiam*, to avoid offence; but mine eye and my reputation are two such tender things, as being touched, Nature bids me defend the one, Honour the other. In doing this, I shall deliver nothing but truth for my Vindication, and that as inoffensively as I can, with that temper that Otho recommended to his nephew Salvius Cocceianus, neither remembring too much, nor forgetting altogether.

<small>Ecclus. xxxii. 2.</small>

<small>Hist. Tripart. l. viii. c. 1.</small>

<small>Tacit. Hist. l. ii.</small>

It

It is a great difadvantage to me, that I know not what to plead in my own defence, becaus I cannot come to know, in any certain way, what is in allegation againſt me. *Adeo factor innocens ſum*, I may ſay, with Cremutius Cordus; and more, I am ſo clear from any matter of fact, that there is not ſo much at preſent, as any criminal word laid to my charge, as not ſo much as a dream, as was of old objected againſt a Gentleman of Rome in Claudius his time (what any man hath dreamt to my prejudice, as it was in the caſe of Silanus, that I cannot yet underſtand). Only this I hear, as the voice of many waters, and as the noiſe of mighty thundrings, a confuſed loud report (but owned by none), That from the time I quitted my employment in the field, I took leave of my firſt principles, and deſerted the Godly party, ſiding with thoſe who had the peſtilent tokens of malignancy upon them. That I have carried myſelf as an enemy to the Army,

Tacit. Annal. l. iv.

Sueton. in Claud.

Dio. l. lv.

Army, Parliament, and Kingdom, by endeavouring to berak the Army, to force the Parliament, and to kindle a new flame of warr in the Kingdome. That upon the failing of these designs, I withdrew beyond sea, transporting great summs of mony, which I had gotten in the warr; and that during my abode in Holland, I took a commission from the Prince of Wales, and was interested in the revolt of the shipps, and in the drawing the Scottish army into England.

These are the arrows, even the bitter words, that are shott against me; so farr as I have been able to learn news of myself. But I thank God they are headless ones, and I shall not fear their impression.

In the first place, to clear myself from the imputation of apostacy, I must crave leave to signify what those grounds and principles were upon which I was originally drawn to engage in the service of the Parliament; that so others measuring them

them with my present actings, and com- 2 Cor. x. 12.
paring me with myself *(me cum meipso)*
which they may better do then I, it may
appear whether or no (according to that
expression of the son of Sirach), I have Eccluf. ii. 13.
gone two ways. My principles (I may
speak it freely and truly) were grounded
upon the publique interest, and had no
other ends than what are laid down in the
declarations of Parliament, and the national
league and covenant; that religion might
be reformed and mainteined; the person,
dignity, and honour of the King preserved,
and the peace and safety of the kingdom
settled: and according to these points (I
may say without vanity) I constantly
steered my course, both in field and Parliament, without allowing myself the least
variation. The warr I abhorred, though I
acted in it, as upon the defensive (which
I thought justifiable), but it was ever with
a wish, that the sword (as it was fabled of
Hercules his) might be dipt in oyl, rather

B 4   than

then in blood; that the difference might end, rather in a peace than a conqueſt; that (as it fell out in the deciſion between Zenocles and Euripides) the one party might not have the worſe, nor the other the better; but ſuch an accommodation might take effect as might be with ſaving of honour to King and Parliament, whereby both might have the beſt. *Victor uterq.* And from this conſideration it was, not from any baſe or treacherous compliance, (as ſome have been pleaſed to ſuggeſt) that ſo long as I held any employment in the armies, I conſtantly endeavoured to expreſs all the civilities I could to thoſe of the adverſe party, that ſo our differences might be kept in a reconcileable condition; and we might ſtill look upon one another, according to Ariſtotle's rule, as enemies that might live to be friends. The ſame inclination ledd me even in the time of my engagement, and upon all occaſions afterward, to the laſt minute of my ſervice in the

Margin notes:
Ælian. Var. Hiſt. l. ii. c. 8.
Martial.
Ariſtot. Rhet.

the House of Commons, to vote for propositions, and to endeavour a fair closure with his Majesty; but still *salva integritate*, and without the least forfeiture of my principles; so that I may say, *Et hoc volui, et etiam institutum servare.* Epictet. Enchir.

It is true, in the subdivision of the Parliament I may possibly be represented as not so constant and firm in my station, having at first sided with that party, which is now declared independential, and since, with the other known by the name of Presbyterian, which may have given occasion to that second aspersion cast upon me, that I quitted the Godly party, or at least seemed so to do, like a falling starr,

Quæ si non cecidet, potuit cecidisse videri. Ovid. Metamorph. l. ii.

But I hope I shall make it appear to all indifferent and impartial judgments, that when I was thus minded I used no lightness; it was not *etiam, etiam, & non, non.* This change was not in me, but in others; 2 Cor. i. 17.

or

or if in me, yet occasioned by the alteration and change of others; *tanquam accidens per aliud,* or (as I may say) *accidens per accidens.* I desire not to be an accuser of those whom I have formerly looked upon as my brethren: most confident I am there be many saints among them, truly so called; and it is a misery to think, and may be a lamentation to consider, that there should be saints on two sides, and those so divided that, like parallel lines, (though both right and straight) they cannot be brought to meet and concenter together. But yet I am of opinion, that all are not of the godly party that wear that badge, and cognizance; all are not burning that are shining lights among them. There is *putredo lucens*; rotten wood may shine. I am sorry to see how small a piece of religion will serve to make a cloak; and ashamed to think how som have worn it to cousin others.

At

At the firft, in the beginning of thefe fatal troubles, before they quartered any diftinction, they were not vifible, but went in the crowd among thofe honeft men that ftood for the intereft of religion and liberty; only they were remarqued for their extraordinary diligence and activity to advance and promote the fervice, which knitt my heart to them. But fince that, I am well affured, many of them have not walked uprightly, according to the truth and fimplicity of the Gofpel; but rather like *boutefeux*, and incendiaries, putting the whole ftate into combuftion and confufion; and this alienated me from them, and I fhall not be carefull to anfwer them in this matter. I think it may be enough for me to fay, that I ufed them as Mofes did his rod; fo long as they were of aid and fupport to the Publique I inclined to them, and refted in fom meafure upon them; but when I faw they had tragedies in their hearts (as Dionyfius painted Ariftarchus)

tarchus) and that they deviated from what they had publiquely professed before God and the world, into impious, disloyal, antimonarchical ends; when I saw them turn serpent, I thought it time for me to fly from them. Neither was I the only person that parted with them at this turning; for I could name very many, and those of eminent reputation for piety and integrity, Members for both the Houses, who, with an abhorrency and perfect detestation of their actings, did at the same time bid them farewell, as well as I. So that I am induced by hope (the common flatterer) to persuade myself, that all dispassionate and disinterested persons will free me from that imputation of levity, which some would stick upon me, as if I were but desultor (as they called Deillius) a skip jack from one side to another, without any mature consideration; when they be pleased to see that I hold the same foundation I did at first; and that I changed my company

pany, but not my mind; that indeed those people left me, and not I them.

But it is objected, as a point of folly and weakness in me, that in this change I quitted my friends to joyn with those whom I knew to be my mortal enemies. To this I must answer, as I said before, that I did not quitt them, nor desert my friends, but kept on in the same constant road, sweetning counsail with them, in order to the establishment of peace and truth: but they left me, and took into that wilderness of their own inventions, wherein they have lost both themselves and us, when we had but a short step to make unto, and were indeed upon the border of a promised happy reformation. I confess, after that defeat which I received at the Devizes, upon my return to London, I found (contrary to my expectation) a multitude of friends (so called) *populum amicorum*, in the Independent party that appeared for me. In that heat (as the sun is ever hottest

Sen. de Benef. l. i. c. 33.

test after a cloud) I had an offer from them of a very confiderable army to be raifed, and putt under my command, with a conftant maintenance for it, if I would engage myfelf to entertein none but godly officers, fuch as fhould be recommended to me. Unto which I replied, that I defired nothing more than to have fuch officers about me, as might be remarkable for that fpott, as Mofes calleth it; but I wifhed them to confider, that there went more to the making up of an officer than fingle honefty. *(Alia ratio boni civis, & boni viri,* as Ariftotle faid in another cafe). A good man might make a good fouldier, but there muft go the good man and the good folldier to the compofition of a good officer. I befought them likewife to weigh my condition, how I ftood anfwerable with my life and honour, for any mifcarriage that fhould fall out in the fervice, and that it would be a poor plea for me to fay, it was the officer's fault, when it might be juftly

Deuteron. xxxii. 5.

Arift. Ethic. l. v. c. 2.

juftly retorted upon me as my fault that I took fuch officers. This I affured them; that where I could find perfons qualify'd with piety and ability (fuch faithfull centurions as knew how to command, and when to fay, go, come, do this) I would preferr them before all others. But in the want of thofe I looked to be excufed, if, for the advantage of the fervice, I made bold to employ fuch as fhould appear to be able fouldiers, although they were not otherwife fo refined men as I could wifh. And to the end that there might be a fair choice, and to obviate all exceptions (the Parliament having voted a confiderable body to be raifed for me), I appointed a council of warr, whereof Sir Arthur Hefilrigg was prefident, to examine the merits of every man that fhould ftand to bear any office in that army, with power to crofs all fuch out of the lift as fhould be judged unfitt or unworthy to be employed. But this did not fatisfy; and I then found they had

it

it in their defigne to modell and form an army, that fhould be all of their owne party, and devoted to their own ends. Upon this we differed. I trufted not them, nor they me, and fo we agreed. From that time forward I may date the expiration of their friendfhip.

It is true that long after (and fo long indeed as I held my command) I was kept up by them: but I could plainly perceive it was but in the nature of a ftale, in oppofition to that noble Lord the Earl of Effex, whom they feared, and therefore hated implacably: and they were willing enough to foment thofe differences between his Lordfhip and me (to the prejudice of the public fervice), that they might make their ends upon us both, and gain the better pretence to bring on their new modell. In what condition I was mainteined, may be demonftrated by the treafurer, Mr. John Trenchard his accompts, where it will appear, that from the time

of

of my setting forth unto my disbanding, I
never received full one hundred thousand
pounds (an inconsiderable summe, compared
with what others had); and yet out of
that stock, I was fain to play the good
husband, and to be at the charge to pay
for part of my arms and ammunition. Besides this, they would be sure I should
never have an entire body of my own; but
so compounded of city and country regiments, that when they pleased they might
take me in pieces, like a clock: and this
was the true reason why I could never improve any successes; because these adven-
titious, borrowed forces, having no depend-
ence upon me, but upon those that sent
them, would not follow me further then
pleased themselves, but would be ready
to march home when they should have
pursued their point, as if they had don
enough when they had don any thing.
Yet such were the charities which I mett
with in the world, that it was made my
fault,

> 2 Kings, xiii. 19.

fault, that like Joash, I gave over shooting sooner than I should have don; when, in truth, I had no more arrows left to shoot. From time to time I was putt upon all disadvantages, that might lessen me in my reputation, and expose me to ruine. Witness, among other particulars, the hopeless employment into the West, as it was rightly stiled by John Lillburn in one of his pamphlets; when I was commanded to march without delay to the relief of Taunton, with a body of horse, and a few dragoons, and a vote for three thousand foot (of which I never received the benefit of one man): and this against a complete formed army, far exceeding my strength, in a deep enclosed country; where it was known, that every field was as good as a fortification, and every lane as disputable as a pass. So that, in effect, I was in no better condition than those gladiators of old among the Romans, preserved awhile, to perish in the end, and kept only

to

to be loft. This was the friendship I parted with. But admitting these people had been my friends never so much; the old rule, *usque ad aras*, is in force still; and I think I should never have been able to answer, either to God, or the world, or mine own conscience, if I had suffered myself to be swayed by any private obligation, further then was consistent with the publick interest. Plato and Socrates, this man and that man, may have been my very good friends; *sed magis amica veritas.*

But I joined with my enemies. *A suo danno*, as the Italian said, when one told him that his hors cutt; at his peril that did it: mine error remaineth with myself. Tob. xix. 4. For that matter, I think it may pass for an evident demonstration, that therein I went according to my conscience; when I engaged in a party, where I could neither meet with affection to blind my judgment, nor expect obligation to captivate my affection. If there were any among them

C 2   that

that were sowered with the leaven of maliciousness against me, and they be yet within the reach and compass of my prayers, the good LORD forgive them: I do, as I humbly desire to be forgiven. This I can say for myself, that in my travel thorough these intrigues, I have desired, and (according to my weakness) endeavoured to keep in ane even way, without wheeling to friend, or from foe. I have neither hated any man's person because of his interest, nor affected any man's interest because of his person: but according to the best of my poor understanding, I have constantly sided with those, be they who they would, *quamvis ignis, quamvis aqua*, whatever were their temper towards me, whom I found adhering to the principles of the covenant, and willing to keep in that road with me.

But it is further alledged, that I have endeavoured to break the Army, to violate the Parliament, and to embroil the kingdom

kingdom in a new warr. Truly if I were guilty of that above mentioned backsliding from goodness, and good men, I should not wonder at all to find myself engaged in these, or in any other treasonable practices; for apostacy is a bottomless gulf, whereinto being faln, it were no less then a miracle if I should not fall infinitly. In such a condition, *Res est stulta nequitiæ modus.* But I hope I have already said enough to clear my integrity, as to that particular, and to shew I have not lost my first love; but that the metamorphosis is in them that would impute this change unto me. True charity is believing, and to that I appeal. For those other imputations, wherein malice and folly concur in the same language against me (as snakes and geese hiss alike), they are but so much noise; *cisterna sonitus,* as David phraseth it; and I doubt not, by the help of God, but to prove that there is nothing but nothings in this all, that is, or can be objected;

_{Sen. Fragm.}

_{1 Cor. xiii. 7.}

_{Psal. xl. 2.}

or,

or, at the uttermoſt, no more than will amount to that, which Vitellius was ſo willing to pardon in Suetonius Paulinus, and Licinius Proculus, the crime of fidelity.

<small>Tacit. Hiſt. l. 2.</small>

Though I ſcorn to court, yet I love not to deſpiſe Fame; I would not be miſrepreſented to the army. God knows I have never been wanting to pay it all juſt reſpect. I acknowledge the great ſervices don by it. I have acted, I have voted for it. The ordinance of indemnity, the votes in favour of apprentices; for proviſion of maimed ſoldiers, widows, and orphans; for exemption from preſs, had every one of them my concurrence; and for the payment of arrears, I may ſay I was for it to the uttermoſt farthing. I may not ſay who were againſt it: but thoſe who ſeemed to be pillars, or ſomewhat (whatſoever they were, it maketh no matter to me) contributed nothing, nay, gave their flatt negative to it. And, truly, herein I did but diſ-
charge

charge my confcience: for I was ever of opinion that a fouldier's pay is the jufteft debt in the world. For if it be a crying finne to keep back the wages of an hireling, that doth but fweat for us: it muft needs be a roaring altitonant finne, to detein pay of the fouldier that bleeds for us. There is a cry of blood in it, and GOD will make inquifition for it.

Deut. xxiv. 15.

Yet for all this I cannot put off the beggar's jewel, Plain-dealing. All that hath been well don cannot juftify, or difannull, what hath been ill don. If a man preferve my houfe from being broken up, and afterwards fet it on fire, fhall the remembrance of that obligation difcharge this offence? I trow not. GOD hath faid it, " The righteoufnefs of the righteous " fhall not be remembered in the day of " his tranfgreffion." I cannot look upon the army with fuch an implicit faith, as Walter Mapes looked upon the Church of Rome, under the notion of a ftaff plunged

Ezek. xxxiii. 12, 13.

plunged under water, which unto the eye may seem distorted and broken, but is entire, right, and straight: so as to conclude with *absit credere quæ videmus*; that I must not give credit to mine own reason, nor believe what I see. Mine eye affecteth my heart. I see, and grieve to see. How is the gold becom dimme? How is the most fine gold changed? They that claim no less, then to be God's host, an army of Saints; that were raised, and engaged both by commission, oath, covenant, and their own solemn protestations and remonstrances, to defend the true Protestant religion, to preserve the King's royal person and dignity, and legal authority, and to maintein the rights, privileges, and freedom of Parliament, and the fundamental laws and government of the kingdome: that were looked upon with so much honour, both at home and abroad, as those that fought for nothing but the things that are JESUS CHRIST's, and fought for nothing

Sam. iii. 51. and iv. 1.

Gen. xxxii. 2.

Phil. ii, 21.

thing but a safe and well grounded peace, they are becom the men that have given great occasion to the enemies of the LORD to blaspheme, by introducing a general confusion in the Church, fomenting Popery, tolerating Heresy, countenancing Schisme, prophaning Holy Ordinances, persecuting good Ministers, and indeed the Ministry, to the shame of Protestants, the joy of Papists, and the joy of Athiests. These are they, that contrary to the known laws of the realme, contrary to the Oaths of Allegiance and Supremacy, and contrary to the Solemn League and Covenant, and the many, many declarations and remonstrances of Parliament, have been made instruments to destroy the person of his late Majesty, and to lay the honour of his royal family in the dust! What shall I say! The greatest griefs are tongue-tied: but it would make a dumbe man speak, like Cræsus his son in the story. These are they, that contrary to the tenor of that Herod. l. 1.
ordinance

ordinance, 15th February, 1644, whereby they were new modeled under the Lord Fairfax, for the defence, among other particulars, of the laws and liberties of the kingdom, and with an obligation to be from time to time subject to such orders and directions as they should receive from both Houses of Parliament, have in their licentious and irregular proceedings disobeyed, invaded, subdued, and broken the Parliament, the only authority whereby they were created, and commissioned an army; and without which they were no better than a great riot. Not to speak of all their mutinies, and practises against it (for that would be *immitere pecus in pratum, ubi non est sepes*; and besides, that I shall have occasion to touch upon them in a fitter place). That renowned act may pass for enough, when they took the liberty to practise physick upon the Houses without a licence. Certainly, if Esculapius were deified only for his invention of purging, and

and tooth-drawing: what immortal honour might these men expect, who have found out the way to purge a Parliament, to pluck out burgesses, and to cut of Lords? (that I say no more). He that sins before his maker, let him fall into the hands of such empirics. *Ecclus. xxxviii. 15.*

It is not to be forgotten, in the account of our unhappy distempers (as physitians reckon in the progress of a disease, *ab actionibus læsis*), that nothing putt the Houses of Parliament into a greater inflammation then that unhappy demand of the Five Members, made by the late King, in the House of Commons, which was interpreted such an horrid violation of privilege, as that although his Majesty were pleased to withdraw the prosecuting of it, and to promise a more tender respect for the time to com; yet, nevertheless, this sparke (as his Majesty terms it) kindled such flames of discontent, as gave occasion, first to the raising of guards, and afterwards to the levying *Εικων Βασιλ.*

vying of an army. If I could have Alfonſo's wiſh, to ſpeak *ex ſpecula aliquâ eminentiſſima*; or ſuch an opportunity as Jotham had upon Mount Gerizim, ſo to deliver myſelf, as I might be univerſally heard, I ſhould addreſs myſelf to the army in the language of Oded, Are there not with you, even with you, ſins againſt the LORD your GOD? The ſame ſins, and greater? Have you not out-acted the King above twenty for one? He demanded but Five Members out of the Houſes, and never took one; you have plucked Two out of the very Houſe of Commons, impriſoned Forty-five, and ſecluded Ninety-eight; and are ſo farr from retracting what you have don, that you ſtill are opinionate, and perſiſt in your way, to the utter ſubverſion of both that, and all future Parliaments. And do you think, who have judged his Majeſty, and yet do the ſame things, and infinitely worſe, that you ſhall eſcape the judgment of God?

Sabellic. Enn.

2 Chron. xxviii. 10.

Rom. ii. 3.

But

But yet there may be a reserve of charity. It may be hoped that the army, though they have failed in their obedience to the Parliament, may have made good their trust to the country, to the freeborn people of England, which is paramount to all other obligations. Indeed they have freed us from King, Lords, and Commons, and from whatsoever was of honour or worth in the nation; and we may brag of the same liberty which the inhabitants of the isle of Corcyra, or Corfu, were proverbially said to enjoy, *carcare ubi volueris*, a man may be free to untruss, where he will. Witness our very churches, so polluted by them, that if Athenodorus were alive again, he might make a judgment of the diseases, and ill habits of this time, *ab excrementis*. To be short, after the expence of so much blood and treasure, all the difference that can be discerned between our former and present estate is but this; that before time, under the

[margin: Erasm. Adag.]
[margin: Strabo.]

the complaint of a slavery, we lived like freemen; and now, under the notion of a freedom, we live like slaves, enforced by continual taxes and oppressions, to maintein and feed our own misery. And this must needs be the more insupportable to all that have any sense of generosity left in them; because it is not an open enemy, that hath don this, but such as were our servants, should be our friends, and have made themselves our masters, or, to use their own stile, our conquerors. So that as the poor woman once sang to her mill, "Grinde mill, grinde, for Pittacus grinds "the Mitylenians;" we may go sing the same ditty, *mutato nomine*, and bemoan our condition under the pressure of the army, whereby our faces are thus grinded, and our estates thus consumed.

Plut in Conviv. sap.

But all this must be borne with patience, as in order to a reformation; of which there cannot be a birth expected in reason, without som pains and travail. I deny not

not, but possibly som things in the frame of our state might be amiss; and in a condition fit to be reformed. But is there no mean between the tooth-ach, and the plague? Between a sore finger, and a gangrene? Are we com to Asclepiades's opinion, that every distemper is the possession of the devil? that nothing but extreme remedies, nothing but fire and sword, and conjuring, could be thought upon to help us? Was there no way to effect this reformation, without braying the whole kingdom in a mortar, and making it into a new paste? Those disorders and irregularities, which through the corruption of time had grown up among us, might, in process of time have been well enough reformed, with a saving to the preservation and consistency of our flourishing condition. But the unbridled violence of these men hath torn our head from our shoulders, and dismembred our whole body, not leaving us an entire limb. *Inq; omni* Martial, l. 1. ep. vii.

omni nusquam corpore corpus. Like those indiscreet daughters of Peleus, they have cutt our throats to cure us. Insteed of reforming, they have wiped, though not yet cleansed the kingdom, according to that expression in the Scripture, as a man wipeth a dish, and turneth it upside down: And in lieu of preserving the supreme authority, they have left us nothing but a representative of a representative, a shadow of a dream, a nothing of nothing. *Tota domus duo sunt.* The Lords I know, and the Commons I know; but who are ye? The good spirit might have asked the question.

But yet for all this, *bona verba,* what they have don, though confessed to be in itself irregular, and not justifiable, they have been enforced to do it; and necessity, which is *lex temporis,* as it putt them upon it, so it must bear them out in it. Besides, they had wonderfull good intentions; which being added to the case of necessity, could not but make up a considerable plea,

Causa

[margin: Ovid. Met. l. 7.]
[margin: 2 Kings, xxi. 13.]
[margin: Ovid. Met.]
[margin: Seneca.]

Causa necessitatis & utilitatis æquiparantur in jure. To this, they that suffer the wrong, may have leave to ask the question, Who made the army a judge over us? If they be our inferiors, their obedience is their best sacrifice; if our equals, they are not competent judges, it is *par in parem*; if our superiors, let them produce that great charter, which must be derived either from the authority of King and Parliament, or from the consent of all, or at least the major part of the people of England. As for the honesty of their intentions and ends, we can judge of it no otherwise then as we judge of the tree by the fruit, by their declarations and actions, and they have been many times, as contradictory one to another as blessing to cursing, sweet water to bitter. Witness that agreement of the people, declared in November 1647, and their disagreement from it, published shortly after. As likewise their repentance of their disobedience, so formally

Abb. Panormit.

formally profeſſed at Windſore, and their acting the very ſame again at London, almoſt with the ſame breath, as if to ſhew that they repented that they had repented. My brethren, theſe things ought not ſo to be.

<small>Jam. iii. 19.</small>

And for that lawleſs neceſſity, which they pretend, whereby they were enforced to take the way of the ſword to cut thoſe knots which they could not otherwiſe untie; it may juſtly ſeem ſtrange, that being ſo extreme and invincible, it ſhould be inviſible and imperceptible, like thoſe atoms which Democritus held to be diſperſed through the whole frame of the world, but no body could ſee them; or like that Pythagorean harmony of the ſpheres, which was ſaid to be excellent muſique, but nobody could ever hear it. What fury ſoever it was that inſtigated them to act theſe violences ſo freely againſt their wills, *ultro, ſed animo invito*, as Cedren expreſſeth it out of Homer; certain it is, that all was quiet among us, untill their drumms began to rattle;

<small>Cedren Hiſt. p. 632.</small>

rattle; the winds were laid, the earthquake settled, the flames amortized and extinguished, which accompany'd our former troubles; and there appeared no cause, but that we might hope that GOD was coming to us in the still and soft voice of Peace. The necessity alledged by them may seem, in the operation thereof, to have something of the virtue of the philosopher's stone, which is said to have contrary effects: for in June and July 1647, it wrought a treaty with the late King, accompanied with a remonstrance, that there could be no firm or lasting peace without a due consideration of, and provision for his Royal family and party: they are their own words. And in November 1648, it raised those humours that vented themselves against all accommodation with his Majesty, and broke out into violent effects against the Parliament, upon no other account but because the Houses had entertained a personal treaty with him. So that *super totam materiam*, they make themselves judges of this necessity, and retein a kind of episcopal jurisdiction over it, *potestatem ligandi, & solvendi*, to make it fast or loose, according to their own good will and pleasure.

Did not the late King make use of these very arguments in the case of shipmony? That he would not seek to levy it but when he should be necessitated by som imminent danger, and then with no other intention but for the public defence? And yet the Parliament decried it, as introductory to an arbitrary government; and, as so, declared against it. But that is too good a parallel case: worse a great deal may serve the turn, and it may befitt these people better. May not a felon at the bar plead as much, and with as much reason say, his necessity compelled him to take a purse, and he intended only to relieve his wants? I need not put the question, whether the jury would acquit him upon it, it, or no. But whatever the folly, or wickedness of wit can invent, neither necessity nor honest intentions can make that straight which is crooked: no excellency of speech, no words of man's wisdom, though never so enticing, will be able to justify the breaches of faith, and violations of duty; no not the least evil, though in order to the greatest good. Will ye speak wickedly for GOD, and talke deceitfully for his cause? Saith Job—*Non defensoribus istis*—Certainly, according to these principles, all fences and inclosures of Government are plucked up, and laid open, and according to Lysander's justice (the longest sword will be the measure of the best cause). Pretences will never be wanting against any authority, so long as ambition may beget a necessity, and coveteousness a well-meaning, to make good the force. At this rate those gentlemen of the army may com to be paid in their own coyn, and the retaliation just before GOD: for

Ecclef. i. 15.

Plut Lacon. Apo.

as they, upon the forementioned grounds, have taken the liberty to invade the Parliament; so may any other army, upon the same square of reason, presume to fall on 2.Sam.ii.26. upon them, Will it not be bitterness in the end?

I would not in all this be misunderstood, as if I criminated the whole army; GOD forbid that I should condemn the righteous with the wicked. I know well there were many persons of integrity and gallantry in it, whose souls were vexed with those proceedings; who, though they were of that body, yet were not of that minde, but were necessitated to hold with it, only because in this calamitous time they knew not how to subsist without it, reteining such a kind of slippery interest in it as, like a piece of ice, they could with no certainty hold, or part with. Those I am confident would, upon a good occasion, shew themselves ready to act according to the rules of honour and conscience. And therefore I have

have a refervation of a due refpect for them. Neither do I, in that peccant party, condemn all alike: for I do verily believe there were many honeft malefactors among them, that were led into this engagement, like thofe men of Jerufalem that followed Abfalom, in their fimplicity, 2.Sam.xv.11. knowing nothing. Thefe I commiferate. But the woe be upon thofe by whom the offences are com; who acted thefe poor men to their own ambitious ends, and blinded them with falfe pretences, as the Philiftines blinded Samfon, only to make them grinde their grift; fporting at them when they have don their work; or paying them for it with a mufquet-fhot in the head. O my foul, com not thou into their fecret; unto their affembly, mine honour, be not thou united: I cannot but look upon thefe men with horror and abomination, as engaged beyond the hope of a retreat; as reduced to that miferable neceffity of being wicked; and therefore in the condition of

that

that Lacedemonian, when he clap'd an oyster into his mouth, shell and all; resolved to swallow what they have begun to chew: I take my leave of them, with Michaiah his farewell to Ahab, Go and prosper. For their comfort, they have but two enemies, GOD, and all good men.

But it is still urged, that before the army had contracted this guilt, and when it was in a state of innocency, I acted the part of a serpent, by my endeavours to destroy it, practising at Saffron Walden, and elsewhere, to divide and disband it, and raising prejudices and jealousies against it in the House of Commons, to the hindrance of the relief of Ireland, and the hazard of the safety of England, and therefore the fire that afterwards broke out in it was of my kindling and blowing.

For answer whereunto I desire it may be remembred, that after it had pleased our good and gracious God to stop the bleeding veins of this kingdom, by determining

Athen. Dipnos. l. iii.

mining the late more-then-civil-warr, there being then nothing of hoſtility left in the field, all ſwords ſealed up (as it is written to have been in Pompey's army, though upon another account) and all garriſons reduc'd, the Scottiſh army withdrawn, his Majeſty's perſon ſetled at Holmby, in order to the ſending of propoſitions unto him, for the concluding a ſafe and a well grounded peace, all things ſeeming to concurr, as in an happy conſtellation, to the re-eſtabliſhment of our ſhaken foundations; it was then held fitt by the wiſdom of the Parliament, to alleviate the burthens and preſſures which the neceſſity of thoſe foregoing times had impos'd upon the kingdom, whereby the people might com to enjoy the fruit of that peace, which, with the expence of ſo much blood and treaſure, they had planted. In purſuance of that end, many things were propoſed; but the reducement of the forces was reſolved upon, as the *primum urgens.* Whereupon
it

Plut. in Pomp.

it was ordind by both the Houses. That the standing army, for the defence of this kingdom, should be contracted to the proportion of ten thousand foot, and five thousand fower hundred horse. That out of the supernumeraries there should be seven regiments of foot, fower of horse, and one of dragoons compleated, and sent for Ireland; the remainder, upon the receipt of two month's pay, to be disbanded; and that, for the maintenance of the forces established, there should be an assessment of threescore thousand pounds a' month laid upon the kingdom of England, and dominion of Wales.

The manner how those forces design'd for Ireland should be drawn out was order'd to be referred to the Committee for the Affairs of Ireland at Derby house. Whereupon the Committee resolved, that the Lord Wharton, Sir John Clotworthy, young Mr. Saloway, and myself, should be desir'd to go to the head-quarter at Saffron Walden,

Walden, with inſtructions (according to the power given by the Houſes). That we ſhould conferr with the generall, or ſuch officers of the army as we ſhould think fitt to communicate with, touching the carrying on of that ſervice, with the greateſt expedition that might be. Upon this, and no other ground, and by theſe degrees, I came to be engaged in that buſineſs of Saffron Walden. And what have I now don? is there not a cauſe? As David ſaid to his angry brethren, when his father had ſent him upon an errand to the army, I did not run before I was ſent; neither was I ſo forward, as to ſay with Ahimaaz, I pray thee let me run. For the truth is, I doubted I ſhould but blow into a waſp's neſt, and ſting mine own lipps. But the Committee, in purſuance of the votes of the Houſes, was pleaſed to command my ſervice, and I look'd upon that as a ſufficient juſtification of my obedience. But I may be, the queſtion will not be ſo much upon

1 Sam. xvii. 29.

2 Sam. xviii. 19.

upon my going, when I was bid to goe, as upon my acting: When it was said unto me, do this, whether I did what I was commanded? Whether the report of those transactions were clearly and fairly made? And whether I did not misrepresent the proceedings of the army to the House of Commons? For satisfaction of these qæries, I shall deliver in a particular account of all my proceedings in that negotiation. And if that plain dealing will not serve to clear me, let me perish like the ermine, in a fair way; rather then I will runn into the dirt to save myself.

March the 20th, 1646, Sir John Clotworthy and I came to Walden, whither Mr. Saloway followed us the next day; but my Lord Wharton declined the business, and came not at all. That evening we made application to the generall, and communicated our business unto him; whereupon immediately he gave order for a convention of the officers the next day. In the

the mean time, according to the latitude given us by the Committee, we took occasion to found the affections of those officers and gentlemen that did us the honour to visit us, how they stood inclined to the service of Ireland, declaring unto them upon what terms the Parliament offer'd that employment. Some we found willing to engage in their own persons. Others, that were not at that time prepared to give a positive resolution did, notwithstanding, assure us of their ready concurrence to advance the business by all possible means. But we mett with a strong spirit of contradiction in very many; som general officers, others persons of eminent quality in the army: who, though they could not have the confidence to speak any thing simply in opposition to the relief of Ireland, yet they made a shift to figure lions in the way, and to obstruct the service by proposing difficulties and unreasonable demands.

The

The next day, the officers being (according to appointment) convened, we delivered our meſſage unto them; after which, they deſired us to withdraw, that they might take into conſideration what anſwer to return. They were not long to ſeek for it; and the reſult was, That they were not, for the preſent, in a capacity, to give their poſitive reſolution, whether they would engage for Ireland, or no; until it were declared, Firſt, what particular regiments, troops, or companies of the army, were to be continued in the ſervice of this kingdom. Secondly, under whoſe conduct, or command in chief, they ſhould go, that did engage for Ireland. Thirdly, what aſſurance they ſhould have of pay, and ſubſiſtence during their employment there: And, Fourthly, that they might have ſatisfaction in point of arrears, and indemnity for their paſt ſervice in England. But however they ſhould think fitt to diſpoſe of themſelves, they undertook in their ſeveral

veral places, to act as farr as they were able, to the furtherance of the service, among those that were under their respective commands.

This way of answering propositions with propositions edified us so little, that we could not choose but desire there might be a second call of the officers, in hope, that upon their recollected thoughts, we might gain a more satisfactory answer from them. Accordingly, the generall appointed a meeting the day following: but the conclusion thereof was, That they could find no cause, either from the votes and resolutions of the House of Commons, or from any other consideration, to alter, or recede from what they had determined the day before.

This positiveness did the more amaze us; because we could see so little ground for it. For as to the point of their pay, the House, in that forementioned vote of the 16th of March, had (as we conceived) made

made sufficient provision: the reality whereof might appear, both in the care that was taken, for the orderly levying of the assessments in the several countries, according to the proportions observed in the ordinance for Sir Thomas Fairfax's army; and likewise in the choice that was made of Commissioners to manage the business, who were the same persons then remaining alive, that were nominated in that ordinance, and known to be faithful to their interest. So that we could not but suspect there were more then Providence in this caution; and truly we were to seek for a good sense in their other demands. That inquiry, what particular forces were to be continued here, putt us into a doubt, that their zeal to the service of Ireland was of but a cold complexion, when insteed of a chearfull declaring, who would go, the first question came to be, who should stay? As if they that could not tell how to stay, might do best to go. And that which made

made it worfe, was the unfeafonablenefs of irrefolute and dilatory counfells at fuch a time, when all the light that GOD had left us in the poor kingdom, was but as a lampe defpifed (to ufe Job's phrafe), appearing now and then in little blazes and fucceffes, *Quafi mox emoriturae lucernae fupremus fulgor*: fo that, in effect, it was no better, then a putting out of the lampe, not to fupply it with oil; it was a quenching of the fpirits of our party there, not to expedite a relief unto them. It feem'd to us a prefumptuous anticipation of the votes of the Houfes, and, at the beft, a curious impertinency in them to queftion under whofe command they fhould go, when the Parliament had not thought fit to declare it. He that afked what was in the covered bafket, was well anfwered, that it was therefore cover'd, becaufe he fhould not know it. There is a certain thing, which Tacitus calls *gloria obfequii*, that befitts an army; Job. xii.

Plut. de curiof.

Tacit. Annal.

army; and, therefore, if it should have pleased the Houses to constitute and appoint a Corporall to have been their Generall, it would have been their duty to accept him, without saying *Nolumus hunc*. In the point of their arrears, they might have taken notice, that there was the same rule of equity held with them, that was observed with all others that engaged for Ireland; and any indifferent reason might judge, what a stone of offence it must needs have been to those that had endured the burthen and heat of the warr, and thought themselves well paid with a penny; if others, that were to come at the eleventh hower, should have the priviledge to receive their two pence. I confess, they reason to demand an act of indemnity, if for no other reason, but because they had made these demands. But we desired not to stretch ourselves beyond our line, and therefore moved no further.

That evening we had information given us

us from very good hands, that there was a petition of dangerous confequence, pretended to com from the fouldiers, but framed and minted by fom of the principal officers, which that afternoon had been tendered to the Convention (in the Generall's own houfe, where he quartered) to be approved, and made paffable and currant by their ftamp; and that it was there preffed with fo much paffion, that an officer of quality, and eminent merit (by name Quarter-mafter-general Fincher) offering his fenfe againft it, was reproach'd by Colonell Rich, as a perfon not deferving to live in the army. Upon this notice, Sir John Clotworthy, and myfelf (Mr. Saloway being then gon away before us to London) refolved, both for our own exoneration, and for prevention of that guilt which might be drawn upon the whole army, by fuch an accurfed thing, to acquaint the Generall with it. We did it; and received this anfwer from him, that he he had not yet heard of any such petition; that nothing of that nature, or tending to that sense, could gain access to the Parliament, but that it must pass through his hands; and that it should be his care to suppress whatsoever might give offence. Upon this assurance, we took our leaves of him, not without hope that having foreseen this basilisk, we had killed it.

But, contrary to our expectation, we were no sooner com to London, but the coppy of the petition was sent up after us, with these representations annexed. First, that whereas the necessity and exigency of the warr had put them upon many actions which the law would not warrant, nor they have acted in a time of settled peace; there might be made (before their disbanding) a full and sufficient provision for their indemnity and security, in all such cases by ordinance of Parliament, unto which the Royal Assent should be desired. Secondly, that Auditors, or Commissioners, might be be speedily appointed, and authorized to repair to the head quarters of the army, to audit and state their accompts, as well for former services, as for their service in this army; and that, before the disbanding of the army, satisfaction might be given to the petitioners for their arrears; that so the charge, trouble, and loss of time, which they must necessarily undergo, in attendance, might be prevented, and that no officer might be charged, in his accompt, with any thing that did not particularly concern himself. Thirdly, that those who have voluntarily served the Parliament in the late warr, might not hereafter be compelled by press, or otherwise, to serve as souldiers out of the Kingdom; nor those who had served as horsmen, be compelled by press, to serve on foot, in any future case. Fourthly, that such in the army as had lost their limbs, and the wives and children of such as had been slayn in the service, and such officers and souldiers as had

had fufteined loffes, or been prejudiced in their eftates, by adhering to the Parliament, or in their perfons by ficknefs, or imprifonment under the enemy, might have fuch allowances and fatisfaction as might be agreeable to juftice and equity. Fifthly, that till the army was difbanded, as aforefaid, fom courfe might be taken, for the fupply thereof with mony, whereby they might be enabled to difcharge their quarters: that fo they might not, for neceffary food, be beholding to their enemies (or, as it was in the printed paper, the Parliament's enemies) nor burthenfome to their friends, nor oppreffive to the country, whofe prefervation they had always endeavoured, and in whofe happinefs they would ftill rejoice.

We were likewife herewithall informed, that both the petition and the reprefentations were promoted in the army, and had already been tender'd to divers regiments, to be fubfcribed; with order, that all fuch as refufed

fused to sett their hands should be cross'd out of the muster-roll. That those regiments, that were quartered remote, had a commandment sent them to draw towards the head-quarters in order to a general rendezvous; and that the whole designe was carried on by Lieutenant Generall Hammond, Commissary General Ireton, Colonel Lillburn, Lieutenant Colonel Pride, and som others. At the same time, we received also a declaration of those officers that dissented from the petition, dated the two and twentieth of that instant March, wherein they nobly shewed their readiness to advance the service for Ireland, modestly representing such inducements as, they conceived, might soonest engage the souldiery. And for whatever might concern their own particular interest, they referred themselves wholy (without any capitulations) to the wisdome and care of the Parliament. This was subscribed by a very considerable number of officers of
the

the field, and others; and came then very opportunely to let the world see, there was no such universal concurrence in the petition, as was afterward very falsly and impudently suggested.

When we were to make a report, Sir John Clottworthy made choice to present the coppies of the petition and representations to the House. For my part, I profess, I was never in my life in a greater dilemma what to do; sometimes I thought I would take heed unto my ways, that I might avoid offence: but when I considered, that in so doing I might keep silence even from good, my sorrow was stirred, and my heart waxed hot within me; and I resolved, according to that obligation of honour and conscience, which lay upon me, to give a true and faithfull account of all that fell within the compass of my lot to report; which I did accordingly, in the other particulars mentioned, sticking the guilt of the whole designe, upon the person

son of Commissary General Ireton, and the rest of the above named officers. It fell out that the Commissary General was not in the House when I made the report; and therefore, there being no officer of the army present that could knowingly, or would willingly speak to these passages, there was no immediat resolution taken; and the rather, because unto that particular concerning the tender of the petition to the several regiments of the army, to be subscribed by the souldiers, there was but a single proof (though avowed by Colonel Harley); so that the House remained in that doubt, which the Schoole termeth a doubt of admiration and astonishment, not of unbelief; and between both determined nothing.

Aquinas.

About half an hower, or an hower after, and during this hesitation, Commissary Generall Ireton came in, and thereupon immediately the House called me up, and commanded me to my report again; and
I did

I did it as before, *iifdem terminis*. The Commiffary Generall, in anfwer to this, told the Speaker, that he prefumed, and took it for granted, that what I had delivered was by way of an information given me, and not as upon mine own knowledge, and therefore he would have nothing to fay to me. But for the matter fuggefted, he was there to avow, that it was a pure fiction, and there was no fuch petition at all, nor any fuch thing in agitation. This being fo confidently fpoken, and by a perfon of that quality and truft in the army, the Houfe continued in a great fufpenfe, untill it pleafed the providence of God to order it fo, that in the midft of the debate (unknown to me, and, I think I may fpeak it confidently, unknown to any body elfe within thofe walls) there came a letter to Col. Roffiter from his major out of Lincolnfhire, fignifying, that a petition had been fent to him from the head-quarters, to be fubfcribed by the regiment,

with

with directions, that he should return their subscriptions to Commissary General Ireton, and the rest of the officers formerly named by me. The concurrence of this second information served, like Eunomus his grasshopper, to supply that string that was wanting in my report, and made up a full evidence of the truth of what I had delivered, so that the House rested satisfy'd with it. Upon this, when som moved, that there might be a vigorous course taken to suppress the petition, the Commissary Generall stood up, and humbly besought the Speaker, that he would not go that way to work, for some reasons, which, if the House commanded him, he should express. The House thereupon required him to speak. He said, Why then, Mr. Speaker, I must confess there is such a petition, and agreeing with that coppy, which hath been presented to you; but both myself and the other officers were necessitated to yield to it, to prevent a worse.

Strabo ex Timeo.

worse. Therewithal he told them of a great inflammation in the army, and that there was no course to be held for the allaying of it, but by a gentle and tender proceeding. This blowing hot, and cold, with the same breath, and in the face of such an Assembly, was entertained with wonder enough.

But the House rested not so; but being justly apprehensive of the rising of this smoak, and desirous to prevent the flame that might follow it, ordered the Speaker to dispatch a letter forthwith to the General, accompanied with a coppy of the petition, requiring him, by the best means he could use, to stop any further proceeding upon it. The informations given in by me, they referr'd to a special Committee to be examined thoroughly: and, for the encouragement of those officers, who by their declaration had signifyed their good affection to the House, and their noble readiness to advance the service of Ireland,

Ireland, they voted, That the House did accept of their engagement, and gave them thanks for it, with a promise, that they should have the same proportion of arrears, and advance, that the others, who had formerly undertaken that employment, had received. To this end they impower'd the Committee fitting at Derby-house for the affairs of Ireland, to treat with them and any other officers of the army, or any whosoever, for the carrying on and perfecting of that service, and to offer the same conditions to them, reporting all to the Houses. This don, to shew the high dislike they had of the petition, that night, after a long debate, they voted a declaration against it, and the representations annexed unto it, as tending to put the army into distemper and mutiny; to impose conditions upon the Parliament, and to obstruct the relief of Ireland; approving their good service who first discover'd it, commending all such officers and souldiers as had

had refus'd to joyn in it, assuring pardon to those who, by the persuasion of others, had been drawn to subscribe it, if, for the future, they should manifest their dislike of what they had don, by forbearing to proceed any further; and declaring, that all those who should continue in their distempered condition, and go on in advancing and promoting that petition, should be looked upon and proceeded against as enemies to the state, and disturbers of the public peace.

This was that declaration that gave the great scandal to the army; and that was afterwards charged to be surreptitiously gotten, at an unreasonable hower of the night, contrary to the intention and direction of the order of the House; contrary to the rules of justice, and usual course of Parliament, when most of the members were departed. I acknowledge it was a night piece; and it was late before it was pass'd; but if that were enough to make

it

it apocryphal, it would reflect upon diverse other votes and orders of the House, (some of the greatest importance) that smelt of the candle as much as this did, and yet, notwithstanding, remain in full force and unquestion'd. How the House could be surprized with it, after so long a debate, is hardly imaginable. Order there was none, to prohibit the bringing of it in that night; only the dissenting gentlemen conceived there would be nothing don thereupon till the next day. If upon this false conception most of the members took the liberty to depart, before the busines was settled, I think the fault was not in the late sitting up of the House, but in their going to bed too soon. Wheresoever the fault was, whether in the House of Commons by night, or in the House of Lords by day, it being becom the Act of both Houses, *factum valuit*.

To quicken this declaration, which of itself might seem but a dead letter, the House

Houſe took a reſolution to print it in ſom examples, and thereupon ſhortly after ordered, that Lieutenant Generall Hammond, Col. Hammond, Col. Lilburn, Lieutenant Colonel Pride, and ſom others (the principal promoters of the petition), ſhould be ſent for up to the barr, to make anſwer for their carriage in that buſineſs. And that thoſe interpoſitions might not eclipſe the relief of Ireland, it was voted, That the Committee at Darby-houſe, for the affairs of Ireland, ſhould have power given them to draw off the forces of the army, that would engage in that ſervice, into a body by themſelves, and to diſpoſe them into regiments, or otherwiſe, as ſhould be held moſt convenient. And that directions ſhould be given to the Generall to quarter the other remaining regiments more at large, and further aſunder one from another; and to ſend his countermand to ſtop thoſe that had received order to march up nearer to the head-quarters.

Die Martis 30, Martii, 1647.

Die Veneris, 9 Apr. 1647.

All

All this was don upon a rational wife confideration, that if the principal firebrands were well quenched, and the coals rak'd abroad and difperfed, the fire would go out of itfelf; and that in drawing thofe Irifh forces into a diftinct body, it would be a good piece of chymiftry to feparate the pretious from the vile, and to divide the interefts of the army; that fo in cafe of a quiet fettlement here, there might be a relief ready prepared for Ireland; or if the difcontented party fhould offer to ftirr, there might be a feafonable provifion for defence.

But notwithftanding all this, leaft the juftice of the Houfe might feem to incline more to the fword then the fcale, it was thought fitt to take the weight of the qære's propofed in the name of the army, that what fhould appear to be reafonably defired, might be fairly granted, thereby to cut off occafion from thofe that defired occafion; and that none might be able to say, that the Parliament, by denying the army a right, had given it a right to do wrong, according to that of the poet, *omnia dat, qui justa negat.* Whereupon these several votes were passed, That the troops in the particular counties of Leicester, of Salop, Chester, Stafford, Warwick, and Northampton, should be conjoyned in one regiment, under the command of Colonell Needham, and be one of the regiments to be kept up in the kingdome of England: and that out of the cavalry of the army, the General's own regiment, Lieutenant Generall Cromwell's (under the command of Major Huntington as Colonell), Colonell Rossiter's (under the command of Major Twisleton, as Colonell), Colonell Greave's and Colonell Whaley's regiments, should be continued upon the new establishment in this kingdome. There was nothing resolved concerning the foot, partly because it could not be then known, what proportion thereof it might

Lucan.

Die Jovis 8, 8 Apr. 1647.

might be fit to referve, in regard it was the defire of moft of the counties (where the garrifons were to be continued) that they might retein their own officers, and fouldiers, who were moft of them perfons interefted in the places where they ferved; and with whom they were already acquainted; and partly, for that there was no fuch mutinous humour then in predomination among the generality of them; but they feemed to ftand in an indifferent fufpenfe, like a pice of iron ballancing between two loadftones of equal attraction, alike inclined (if they were lett alone) either to go for Ireland, or to ftay, or difband at home. And, however, it was conceived, that if the horfe were acquieted, the foot fingly would neither have will, nor power, to do any thing confiderable to the difturbance of the peace.

As to the fervice of Ireland it was voted, That the feven regiments of foot, and fower of horfe (formerly ordered to be sent *Die Martis, 3º Martii, 1647.*

sent into that kingdome) should be taken out of the army. That Major Generall Skippon should command them in chief, under the title of Field Marshall, accompanied with Major General Massey, as lieutenant general of the horse. That there should be an exact list taken of all the forces employed in, or designed for, that service, that were upon the pay of this kingdome, that they might be incorporated in one common enterteinment, upon one and the same foot of account.

*Die Ven. 4°
April.* That the pay of such commanders and officers, as would engage for Ireland, should be higher then of those that were to be continued in England; which was explained by the vote of April the 13th. That the establishment of the officers and souldiers, both those that were already in Ireland, and those that were to go over thither, should be the same with the (present) establishment of Sir Thomas Fairfax's army; and that the proportion of pay, which

was

was to be refpited upon the public faith, fhould be made good unto them upon the conclufion of the warr, out of the rebels lands by Englifh meafure, according to the rates fettled by act of Parliament, fatisfaction being firft made to the adventurers; and that the pay of thofe forces, that were to be kept up in England, fhould be reduced (upon the new eftablifhment) to a lower proportion, according to the particulars expreffed in that ordinance. That, for a further encouragement to thofe forces that engaged for Ireland, the officers fhould all have their debenturs for their arrears, and accounts made up, according to their mufters in their abfence. To conclude, there was an act of indemnity appointed to be drawn up for all, with all the enlargements that could be thought confiftent with honour and juftice. I have been the more particular in the commemoration of thefe votes, to fhew that the Houfes of Parliament were not wanting, on their part, to give all fair satisfaction to the army, if there had been any intention or inclination in them to receive it. But I go on.

Whileſt theſe things were in agitation, there came up a letter from the Generall to the Speaker, bearing date from Walden, March the 30, 1647, wherein he acknowledged the receipt of the order for the ſuppreſſion of a petition, inform'd to be carrying on in the army, in obedience whereunto he had convened all the officers in thoſe parts of the kingdome, and communicated the letter and order unto them. That the officers generally expreſſed a very deep ſenſe of their unhappineſs in being miſunderſtood in their clear intentions, which were no other, then by a petitionary way to repreſent thoſe inconveniencies unto him, which would neceſſarily befall moſt of the army after diſbanding; and thereupon to deſire him to make known, in a ſubmiſſive way, to the Houſe of Commons, so much as he should judge fitt, and seasonable; assuring him, that they would wholly acquiesce in whatsoever he should offer, or the House grant. But he understood not that clause in the Speaker's letter, concerning the marching up of the regiments towards the head-quarters; except it were meant by Sir Hardress Waller's regiment, which was remanded from Newcastle, at the instance of Major General Skippon; and Colonel Hammond's and Colonel Herbert's regiments, which were upon their march from Westchester, being dismissed from that service: that, according to the command of the House, he had sent up Lieutenant Generall Hammond, Colonell Hammond, Colonel Lillburne, Lieutenant Colonel Pride, and Lieutenant Colonel Grimes, to attend their pleasure: concluding, that he trusted the army would ever manifest their affections to the Publick by their constant perseverance in their accuftomed obedience, which fhould ever be really endeavoured by himfelf.

I cannot pafs by this letter, without fom fhort animadverfions upon it: firft, I muft crave leave to admire, that the General fhould be fo unacquainted with the carrying on of the petition, when (as I intimated before), it was openly, and publickly debated, at the convention of officers in his own quarter, and in the room directly under his own chamber, within his hearing; when his own regiment of horfe was fo deeply engaged in it, and appeared in the promoting of it, by an officer of their's fent with a copy thereof to Holdingby, by means whereof fom of thofe forces there were putt into a mutiny: and when one Mofes Bennet (who was employed, the Thurfday before the meeting at Walden, to publifh the petition to Colonel Butler's regiment, with orders for the return of the fubfcriptions unto Lieutenant Generall Hammond,

and

and the rest above named, or any of them, by Saturday March 22d), when he, I say, should presume to avow publickly to the Captain Molineaux, that he undertook that business with the Generall's own consent. Secondly, I cannot but observe the modesty, at that time, of those officers; who professed to look no further in their demands, than to those inconveniencies likely to befall them after disbanding; an act of indemnity; a stating of their debenturs; som consideration of pay, and a little sprinkling of charity, was all they aimed at; but however, the will of the Parliament should be their law, *verecunda sunt initia peccati*. The first essays of sin are veiled, and muffled like Thamax; with continuance men com to act upon the house top, like Absalom. Lastly, for that riddle concerning the marching up of the regiments, the Generall at once disclaims the knowledge of it; and yet resolves it; what he knew not, he knew. Those were

the

the very regiments mentioned (excepting only Colonel Rainſborough's, which was miſtaken, and ſo acknowledged). And if there had been no deſigne in bringing them up, it may be demanded, why they were not ſtop'd in their march, according to the order of the Houſe? But this *de latere.*

Upon the appearance of thoſe officers, ſent up with this letter at the barr, it was expected, that there would have been quick and ſharp proceeding. But the Houſe, having already adjudged the petition, *ſecundum quod erat* (according to the rule, in the judgment of things), was then willing (as in the judgment of perſons it is held beſt), to conſtrue their actions, *in meliorem partem:* and therefore after ſom general queſtions put to them, whereby they might eaſily perceive, there was a greater inclination to believe they were honeſt, then to make them ſo, they were, with a gentle admonition, which was but *irato amore,* diſcharged.

Sen. in Hercul. Oct.

discharged. It is a true observation of Lo. Bacon. that great advancer of learning, that there is no vertue, so often faulty, as clemency. I am sorry to instance, in the favor shewed to those gentlemen; which insteed of softning them, and making them susceptible of good impressions, did but serve to harden their clay temper. For at their return to the army, they stuck not to give out in bravado, that their enemies had don their worst, and that when they came to the barr, there could be nothing produced against them; whereas the truth was, that because the House had thought fitt immediately to discharge them, and had so expressed their sense, therefore there could be nothing produced against them. But the woman apprehended in the act of adultery, was never a whit the more innocent, because nobody prosecuted against her. Those gentlemen might have don well to remember, that they were dismiss'd to their several charges, with a go, and sin no more;

and

and they rewarded evil for good, that turn'd that grace into wantonnefs. It is true there was a great paffion pretended by fom to have the charge againft them verifyed, in order whereunto, there was a fpecial committee appointed to examine proofs; but that committee could never be brought to meet, and when Commiffary Generall Ireton urged to have the evidence produced, with that vain rodomontade, that if it were not don effectually, the informers fhould be accounted the authors, and devifors of fuch fuggeftions, he very well knew, the committee was faln for want of adjournment, and could not deny, but that I moved to have it revived again, although nothing was ordered upon it; and therefore I muft take leave to believe, that both himfelf, and they that feemed to be fuch earneft follicitors for the verification of this charge, did but prefs for the truth, as the frier faid, People feem to prefs for holy water; they would feem defirous to be purify'd with it, but

but if it had com to be dashed in their faces, they would have shrunk at it, *Vero verius ergo quid sit audi, verum, Gallice, non libenter audis.* Martial. l. viii. p. 76.

But I proceed, and my next step must be into Derby-house, where the committee of Lords and Commons for the affairs of Ireland, was pleased, upon the consideration of the votes above mentioned, to lay their desires upon the Earle of Warwick, the Lord Dacres, Sir John Clotworthy, Lieutenant General Massey, Mr. Richard Saloway, and myself; that we would go to Saffron Walden, impowering us by their instructions to treat with the general and officers, to propose, and improve to the best advantage we could, the several votes and orders, for encouragement of those that should engage for Ireland; and as any should accept the service, to draw them into a body from the rest of the army, to dispose them into regiments, or otherwise, and to quarter them in such places, as

should

should be held most convenient in order to their speedy march; and where officers were wanting, to nominate such persons as we should think fitt, and to present them to the committee, to be reported to the House; directing us to give them an account, from time to time, of our proceedings, and to put in execution such further orders, as should com to us from the Houses, or from the said committee.

The 14th of April, 1647, in pursuance of this service, we came all of us (excepting Mr. Saloway) to the head-quarters at Walden, where we were enterteined with informations from several good hands, that there was an evil report brought upon the Irish employment, and that the hand of the commanders and officers was chief in this trespass, from whom a discontented blood had been diffused, and spread into the veins of the army: that the horse were entered into a combination against the service, and great endeavours used to corrupt the

the foot to joyn with them: that in this distemper (as we know, *mota facilius moventur*) there wanted not practices to move, and incite the army against the Parliament itself; some by licentious speeches, others by libellous pamphlets, defaming and blasting it; giving out, that the poor country had paid in their assessments to the Parliament; but the Parliament had diverted the sums to their own private use, and cousened both the country and the army, and that it would be but just to fetch a satisfaction out of their sides; and arraigning the government as unjust, and oppressive, and as acted by a faction; witness that piece (among others), intitled, A Warning for all the Counties of England; divers coppies whereof we found in our inn; which were said to have been brought down in a certein coach from London, to be dispers'd into the several quarters of the army, as afterwards we found *de facto* they were. All that we could do (in that condition),

dition), was but to know, and remember with fom obfervation, that we were likely to meet with foul weather, for the morning was red, and lowring. April the 15th we made our application to the Generall, and having imparted our inftructions, and the votes of the Houfes unto him, we let him know further what we were informed concerning the endeavours to retard, and obftruct the relief of Ireland, and how prejudicial we thought they might prove, if not timoufly ftopped, taking the freedome to offer our opinion, that it might be fitt for him to publifh fomething in declaration of his diflike of thofe endeavours, with a penal commination to fuch as fhould dare to proceed any further in them, and an encouragement to all that fhould either make difcovery of the offenders, or otherwife contribute their pains to the advancement of the fervice. For the faving of time, we fent him that night a draught of a declaration framed to this fenfe, sense, that he might be pleased to signe it, or to make use of the materials thereof, as he should think fittest. In answer whereunto, the General returned an expression of his willingness to promove the service, and of his dislike of any endeavours against it; but he refused to signe any thing of that nature, at that time, in regard it might seem to put a restraint upon the army, and to curb them from speaking their resolutions with that freedom, which was allowed them (the votes only extending to such as should willingly engage), and for that the army was already in som heat, upon occasion of a late declaration; and he feared what a further exasperation might produce. But he promised to speak to the Officers, and to interpose his command to them, that they should not only forbear to cross, but endeavour to advance the service. This return gave us little hope, that there would be any thing material don, either to the clearing obstructions, as to the

Irish

Irish service, or to allaying distempers in the army. That calme reprimende, Why do you such things? and do no more my sons, we know how little it edified; and to think to extinguish a combustion in an army, by allowing the souldiers a freedome to speak their mutinous discontents and passions without restraint, appeared as irrational to us, as if a man should go about, to put out a fire in a furnace, by giving it a vent, which is but the way to make it rage the more.

That afternoon we had a meeting with the officers, where the Generall having by word of mouth declared unto them the substance of what he had intimated to us, as is above mentioned; we caused the several votes and orders of the House to be read; and thereafter my Lord of Warwick, with a great deal of civil language, represented the high estimation which the Houses had of the army, and how thankfully-minded they were of their services, how willing to satisfy

1 Sam. ii. 23, 24.

satisfy their desires in all things, as far as could stand with equity, and the present condition of affairs, encouraging them to embrace the employment offered, as that which was honourable in itself, and should be made beneficial to them. The answer was returned by Colonel Lambert in the name of all (seconded with a cry of, All, All, by some). He desired satisfaction to fower quæres: First, what indemnity they might expect for their pass'd actions? Secondly, what security for their arrears? Thirdly, what establishment for the Irish pay? And, fourthly, who should command that service in chief? Unto which it was reply'd; That as to the first, the House was preparing an ordinance to give full satisfaction, and they might be confident in that particular. To the second and third, that there was provision made in the votes, then communicated to them. To the fourth, that Field Marshal Skippon, and Lieutenant Generall Massey were the persons chosen to command. Som made objection, that they had understood by letters from the Field Marshal, that he desired to be excused from that employment, by reason of his age, and infirmities; and somthing was muttered, but nothing openly spoken against Lieutenant General Massey: I was told afterwards by som of the officers, that Massey was look'd upon as a profane man, and unfitt for a command, where all the congregation was holy. Those that know him, will give him a better certificate, and avow him to be a gentleman of a fair and unblameable conversation: and for his abilities, as a soldier, it were *injuria virtutum*, a kind of discommendation to commend him. Let his own works praise him in the gates. But though he wears a good sword, he cannot bragg of the temper of it, as Thearidas did, of his, that it is *acutior invidia*, sharper than envy. His fault was, that he was not of the faction, which they called the army; and therefore, passing him by

Plut. Lacon. Apoth.

by with a flurr, they com. to this fullen conclufion, that if they might continue under their prefent Commanders in Chief, they would unanimoufly engage. Upon the breaking up of the company we declared, that if any officers had a mind to apply themfelvs to us, we fhould be ready to fatisfy them in all particularities concerning the fervice.

Of all this we return'd an account to Darby-houfe, offering it to their confideration, whether it might not be convenient for their Lordfhips to recommend it to the Generall, that he would publifh fom fuch declaration, as we had formerly tendered to him, giving them the fubftance thereof, according to what is above mentioned: which was fo well approved, that by their letter of the 18th of April 1647, they defired the General to put the faid advice in execution. Upon this importunity, the Generall caufed a letter to be drawn up, agreeable in the matter to what he before had delivered

delivered by word of mouth, and directed it to the Colonells and Commanders in Chief, with order, that it fhould be publifhed, together with the votes of the Houfes unto their refpective regiments. But it was written in fuch a ftile (only as a defire, not as a command), that we could not but apprehend it would prove ineffectual: and fo much we fignified unto him. But his reply was, he hoped, it would operate fully to our ends; and that for the language of it, it was the fame he had ever ufed to his officers, which, as it had formerly, upon all occafions, found a ready obedience, fo he doubted not but it would meet with the like at that time. When we faw this was all we could get of him, we refolved to make trial how we could improve our talent, by our trading with the officers and fouldiers.

For encouragement to the officers, we wrote to the Generall, April the 17th 1647, to defire his order to the Treafurer of the army,

army, that the accounts of all such as would engage for Ireland might be stated. We wrote likewise to the Deputy Treasurer, April the 18th 1647, that from time to time, upon request made by the parties concerned, he should give out certificates unto them, of what was in arrear on their accompt, according to the establishment, and of what remained due unto them, by respit on the publique faith. We made it also our sute to the Generall (when we gave him in the list of those, with whom we had contracted, April 21, 1647) that, in regard those Gentleman had, by their forwardness and example, laid a foundation of encouragement to the Irish service, he would be pleas'd to give them all fitt countenance and respect, whensoever they should have an occasion of address unto him. We gave free enterteinment to all that made us any rational proposition; and to spurr them on the better by hopes of preferment (which is the souldier's whetstone)

stone) where we found the superior officer withdraw, we admitted the next in order to supply his place.

To quicken the souldiers to a speedy resolution, we represented to the Committee, that it might be an advantage to the service, if the Parliament would order the disbanding of all supernumeraries, such as were neither reserved upon the establishment for this kingdom, nor disposed for Ireland; whereby those that could not be taken on here (as few of the foot were likely to be) might be necessitated without any long delays, to cast themselves upon that employment, when they should know there was no other choyse left before them, but either that way, or a discharge. We added our humble advise, in case such a resolution should be taken, that there might be a timely provision made of mony; least, otherwise, if the motion were made to disband, before there were an ability to make satisfaction, we should

but

but stirr ill humors, and not carry them away, which might produce an ill effect. And whereas three weeks pay was then sent down to the army, which, according to a settled rule, was to be distributed, half to the souldiers to supply their wants, and half to the country, to discharge quarters; we proposed, that the moietie designed for quarters, might be allowed to those souldiers that would go for Ireland, as a mark of distinction in point of favor to them, and in consideration both of the charge of their present march into remote quarters, and of the time that might be spent in attending there, for the coming of their two months arrears, which might consume the whole proportion then to be received. We were the rather induced to offer this, because the summe was but inconsiderable to the state, not exceeding three thousand pounds, if allowed for the full number of eight thousand fower hundred foot, and the country might have been satisfied well

enough

enough for the prefent with tickets to be difcounted upon the fouldiers arrears.

Whileft we were fitting thus, at the receipt of cuftome, there wanted no endeavours to obftruct our proceedings; in fome by undervaluing the employment, and fetting the mark of the beaft upon thofe that fhewed themfelvs willing to engage in it; in others, by conniving at thofe ill offices, or (which was worfe) queftioning them but flightly. When thefe little policies would not ferve the turn, it was thought fitt, the Generall fhould be gon, in regard his prefence feemed to be of fo much ufe to our negotiation; whereby we fhould have been left to the fower winds to take our fortune in a difcontented headlefs armie. But before they could fpring that mine, the Generall was defired, by a letter from Darby-houfe of the 18th of April 1647, to refpite his journey till our bufinefs were tranfacted. Upon this failer, the next defigne was to cutt off our line of communication

tion with the officers and fouldiers, as particularly in the cafe of Colonell Lillburn's regiment, where, after we had affigned quarters to fo many companies thereof, as had taken enterteinment for Ireland, under Colonel Kempfon, command was given they fhould forthwith remove into Suffolk, clean out of the road of their march, and to a further diftance from us. But we interpofed in it, and prevailed, that they fhould proceed in their way towards Chefter, in order to their tranfportation.

April the 21ft, after the Generall was gon to London (for longer he would not ftay, notwithftanding that fignification from Darby-houfe), an attempt was made to withdraw thofe fouldiers of Colonell Kempfon's from the fervice, and to put them into mutiny, by one Enfigne Nichols, an officer under Colonell Lilburn; who coming into their quarters (where they lay feparate from the body of the army, by order), there took upon him to publifh the

petition

petition formerly decried by the Parliament, provoking them to demand their pay of their officers in a tumultuary way, and telling them, that if it were refused, they might do well to return to Saffron Walden again; and he would give advertizement thereof to the Generall, and they should have both pay and quarter provided for them. But Captain Dormer (who commanded those companies as Major) discreetly apprehended him, and took the petition and other papers from him, letting us know, that he kept him under guards, until we should send him further directions. Whereupon, weighing the dangerous consequence of such an example, and forasmuch as the fact was committed within the quarters of the Irish forces, we conceived, upon a just ground, that as we had authority to draw those forces off, and to dispose them into distinct regiments and quarters from the body of the army; so we had likewise power to take cognisance
of

of such a misdemeanour, relating to that service within those quarters. And, therefore, in that absence of the Generall, we gave orders to have the said Ensigne sent up to London to the Committee at Darby-house for the affairs of Ireland, to answer the offence there; which was accordingly performed; and upon the report of the business to the House, he was committed by a special order, and those that brought him up in custody were rewarded. The issue of all our negotiation was this, that notwithstanding all interruptions and oppositions divers of the officers relating to ten troops of horse, and fifty companies of foot, were drawn to declare their resolution to engage in the Irish service, upon the conditions propounded by the Parliament; and this account, *in terminis*, we gave in unto the House in our report, without any fallacies or equivocations. They that would dive for a further construction out of those plain terms, as if we had meant, that so

many

many entire troops and companies had actually engaged, did but raife the mud, and obfcure the fenfe of what we delivered.

This was the conclufion of our fecond, and laft employment; and how any thing in all this tranfaction could be fcrewed up to the fignification of an evil defigne, either to break the army, by drawing thofe forces from it, or to obftruct the relief of Ireland, by haftning thofe forces to it, when we acted nothing in reference to either, but according to the ordinance of Parliament, and the inftructions of the Committee, I leave to any impartial eye in the world to judge. And thus, as F. Crefinus (when he was accufed upon a fufpicion of forcery, as if he had bewitched his neighbour's grounds, and charmed the fertility of the foil into his own land), to clear himfelf brought his fhovels, and fpades, and mattocks, with him into the Court, to fhew that his pains and induftry were all the fpells he ufed; I have in like manner

Plin. Nat. Hift. l. xviii. c. 6.

ner thought fitt, to bring in these particular passages for evidence, that I have not endeavoured to fascinate, or blast the honour of the army by any base misreports; nor used any indirect means, to draw away the strength thereof from it; but that I have in a just and fair way taken pains (together with those noble worthy persons) to act according to my orders and instructions: And the Lord God of Gods, the Lord God of Gods knoweth, and I desire the world may know, that in all those proceedings, I have gon on plainly and overtly; and according to that old ceremony (in use when they sacrificed to honour), without veils or masks. If there were any cajolerie or juggling in the business, it was upon their account, that pretended a great zeal to the advancement of the service, and yet, at the same time, possessed the souldiers with an aversation against it, bidding them stick to their arrears, and telling them, the design for Ireland was

Plut. Quest. Rom.

but

was but a trick to break the army. They might juftly be faid, to hinder relief to that poor kingdome, that engaged the fouldiers to declare, that what perfon foever fhould be employed in command, they would not ftirr, until they were firft righted in their fumes and fancies; that cofhiered fuch officers as had fhewed a forwardnefs to that employment, and fell into their quarters that were drawn off from the army, in order to their march for Ireland; taking away their colours, difarming them, and bringing them back again by force; that kick'd and beat others out of the field, and particularly a Major of foot at a public rendezvous, before the General's own face, upon no other ground of exception, but that he had expreffed a fair inclination to that fervice. But I forbear; my prefent tafk leading me rather to clear my own innocency, then to prove others criminal. If in the way of this I may feem to have fhewed any afperity, it is *acetum ex vino dulci,*

dulci, the sharpness of truth: and I shall desire no other charity to pardon it, but that which (according to St. Paul's character), rejoyceth in truth. 1 Cor. xiii. 6.

The next thing, which I meet with objected against me, is, that I should be accessary to those assaults, and almost batteries, that were made upon the houses by the reformado's, souldiers, and apprentices; I affect not recriminations, where, for the most part, the point in issue is but to prove, who is worst. But I must crave leave to wonder at the strength of their complection, that offer to fling the first stone at me for this, who in the same kind are transcendently guilty themselves; who have invaded the city, set guards upon the Parliament, made it unvote itself, imprisoned, secluded, and driven away the members, broken the House of Commons, dissolved the House of Lords, and overturn'd, overturn'd, overturn'd our all. If those actions have tended to assert the

H honour

honour and freedome of the Parliament, and to vindicate it from force and violence, they may be reckon'd, with the square of the circle, *inter scibilia, quæ non sciuntur.* What have I now don, in comparison of them? Is not the gleaning of their grapes, farr beyond my vintage? But I shall make no comparison; because, there is none, between somthing, and nothing. I utterly deny, that I ever had the least hand, either in designing, or acting any of those forcible attempts, and I shall not in this bear record of myself; but appeal to those, that have known me from the beginning of that long fatal Parliament, and before I had the honour to sit in it, when I was but a stander by, and a looker-on upon the world (as Pythagoras stiled himself), a free, disinteressed person, who can witness, and be my compurgators, how much at all times I have abhorred the practise of that popular magick if (I may so call it), those curious arts of conjuring up spirits, som-

times

Aristot.

times in blue aprons, sometimes in white ribbands, to awe, and enforce the Houses, as fatal in their issue, both to the publick, and to the charmers themselvs; who (let them charme never so wisely) do many times run the hazard of Pope Benedict the Ninth, to be torn in pieces by the spirits of their own raising. I shall presume to name, Mr. Speaker, the Master of the Rolls, as in this particular my compurgator, who can testify in my behalf, that upon a certain Lord's day at night, I gave him notice, at his house, of a combination of divers discontented reformado's to affront him, and disturbe the House; and that by my interposition the designe was prevented; and I must acknowledge the right he did me in acquainting the House with it, and the favourable notice which thereupon the House was pleased to take of it. Nay, I might safely appeal to the whole House (with a wish, I would they were sitting), how ready I have been, upon all occasions of this unhappy nature, to employ my endeavours. Witnefs that tumult (among others), when the reformado's, and fouldiers, were gathered together at the door of the Houfe of Commons, and lock'd it, threatning the members, in an infolent manner, if they had not prefent fatisfaction given them. It then pleafed the Houfe to command Mr. Hollis, Sir Philip Stapleton, and myfelf, to go out unto them, and we were the only inftruments to pacify them.

For that bufinefs of the apprentices, wherein (according to the charities of that time) fom perfons would have been glad to faften a guiltinefs upon me, I fhall fhortly repeat, what came to my knowledge of it; and I fhall never go about to brave GOD, with telling a lye, for fear of offending man with telling a truth. It fell out in the time, when, by reafon of the impetuofity of the army, both I, and divers other gentlemen of the Commons, had public leave to withdraw ourfelves, for the

prevention

prevention of that force, that threatned the Parliament through our fides, the particularities whereof will better appear in the following difcours. But as to this matter, the firft air thereof, that, to my remembrance, I ever received, was from a friend of minde (about a fortnight, or three weeks before any thing was publickly known, or acted), who, coming by accident to fee me at my houfe in Drury Lane, took an occafion, by way of difcourfe, to tell me, that he heard, there was a petition preparing in the city, to be tendered to the Parliament. This, I fuppofe, was the fame, that gave occafion to the following tumult: but whether it were fo or no, I cannot pofitively fay: for I do not know, that he ever fpake one fyllable concerning it to me after; and I had no advertifement of it from any, untill the Thurfday before it was prefented; when a fervant of mine, having been abroad upon bufinefs, at his return told me, as the news in the city, that there was

such

such a thing in agitation, and that it was thought there would be many thousand subscriptions to it. The next day it fell out, that I happened to dine with the Lo. Major, who shewed me (as a matter of enterteinment of the time before dinner) a printed Petition; and (if I do not misremember) said, it was the same, that was offer'd to the Common Councill, and had passed there that morning. This was the first, and (I think) the last time, that I ever saw it.

On Saturday, or the Lord's day following (I cannot say certainly which), there came two young men unto me (as I was sitting down to supper) pretending their errand was, to acquaint me with the intention of the City, and Common Council, to present a petition to the Parliament, the Monday morning following, and to desire my advice upon it. I demanded of them, who they were, and they told me, they were apprentices: I reply'd, I knew

no

no advice to be given, but that they would be at Westminster betimes, before the House were pre-engaged in business. But this answer served not their turn, whose end was only to dig a pitt for my soul, and to ensnare me (as I was afterwards sufficiently inform'd); and therefore to draw me on further, they told me, that both myself, and those other impeached gentlemen, were concern'd in this petition: and that they must, and would have us all into the House again, either by fair means or by force. To that, all the return they had from me was, That I would have nothing to do in the business, and so I left them, and went to my company to supper, looking upon them under no other notion, then as wilde, extravagant people; and having no further apprehension of any thing, in regard I heard, the petition was to be brought down by the sheriffs and Common Council, in a regular way, which (I thought) could not have been follow'd

H 4   with

with any diforder. That Monday morning, there came an apprentice to me (who had formerly been with me, about the Ordinance, concerning days of recreation, wherein the Houfe had employed my fervice, and thereby helped me to this cuftome) to let me know, that the fheriffs were gon to Weftminfter with the petition, accompany'd with great multitudes out of the city; and to defire me, that I would be either in Cotton Garden, or in the Hall, that I might be in the way when I fhould be call'd into the Houfe; (for into the Houfe they would have me before they had done). But I flatly refufed it, and defired him, that neither he, nor any elfe among them, would offer to intermeddle in any fuch bufinefs; telling him, if the Houfe had any occafion to command my fervice, they would fignify fo much to me by their order; untill which I fhould have the manners to attend their pleafure.

About an hour after, I had a meffage sent

sent to me from Sir William Lewis, and Sir John Clottworthy, desiring me to come to the Bell in King Street, where we had formerly appointed a meeting to discharge som reckonings, that were due from us to the clerks of the House of Commons. Whereupon I went to Mr. Hollis to advise with him about it. Wee were both very unwilling to have gon, in regard of that concours of people at Westminster: but having notice by a second messenger, that those gentlemen stay'd dinner for us, we could do no less in civility then hold our meeting. At our coming, we found them as much troubled, and perplexed, as we were, and upon the same grounds. To avoid all misconstructions, we fell upon a present dispatch of our business, and resolved but to eat a bitt, and be gon. As we were newly sett down to dinner, there came advertisement to us, that the people were violently broken into the House of Commons; and that they had putt all
things

things into great combuſtion. Whereupon we immediately roſe, paid our reckoning, and departed. And this is the plain, true narrative of all that nothing, which was repreſented in ſuch a magnifying glaſs unto the army. But there is a generation, that have teeth in their tongues (as naturaliſts write of ſom creatures), whoſe words are ſwords, to deſtroy the needy from off the earth, and the poor from among men. O LORD, thou knoweſt, remember me. I hope I have ſaid enough to wipe off this aſperſion (more, I ſhould think would but fret my innocency with over-rubbing it); let it ſuffice me to ſuperadde this proteſtation to what I have ſaid; that if, upon the ſtricteſt inquiry, it can be proved, that I had any acquaintance with the framing, or managing of the aforeſaid petition, or that any way I co-operated in the leaſt degree with the petitioners in their diſorder, I renounce mercy.

<small>Prov. xxx. 14.</small>

In the next place, I finde my ſelf charged with

with the odious name of an incendiary, as if (together with thofe impeached gentlemen) I had endeavoured to levy a new warr in the kingdome, to protect myfelf from the reach of juftice, and to carry on factious defignes. I fhake off this duft in their faces that raifed it, and fcorn any further protection then what mine own innocency, and the juftice and honour of a free Parliament, fhall give me. They that have been acquainted with the paffages of my little world, in the former courfe of my life, can beare me witnefs how little I have affected great things. I may fpeak it truly, and without vanity, I have ever looked upon the fplendent fortunes of the times with a *miferere fœlicium*; and have defired no greater preferment then to be mine own man. GOD hath bleffed me with a competent fortune, and given me a minde (it is his gift) fitted to enjoy that bleffing. In that retired way, I enjoyed myfelf freely, *Nella Signoria di me*, as the Italian fays, in the kingdom of mine

Martial, l. i. ep. 5.

Ecclef. iii. 13.

mine own minde, without other thoughts then such as might arise from quiet senses, looking upon publick affairs, as men use to look upon pictures, at a distance; untill shortly after the beginning of the Long (and I fear the last) Parliament, I had the honour to be chosen into the House of Commons, when I neither sought nor thought of it. What my carriage hath been there, I must submit to censure. I am farr from presuming to justify it (for it was impossible but that my weakness and inexperience must often expose me to disadvantages in so great a Council;) but this I may safely profess, that upon all occasions I acted according to the dictates of my conscience freely, and without ends or interests. I confess, upon the breaking out of the warr (which I look'd upon as *pro aris, et focis*) my passion to the Parliament imbolden'd me to offer my service, as farr as to the raising of, first a troop (when there were but six appointed in all,

and

and it was fomthing to find gentlemen that would engage), and after of a regiment of horfe; and this was all that any man living can fay I fought. Whatever employment of honour I had afterward in that fervice, it was the free will and meer motion of the Houfes (I fpeak with all humble acknowledgment) that put it upon me. And truly, I was fo little fond of the trade of a fouldier (notwithftanding thofe temptations of honour and profitt that accompany'd it), that I gladly gave my vote to the felf-denying ordinance, and the new modell; and when the Committee at Darby Houfe fignify'd their defire to me, that I would continue for fome time in my command, for the profecution of the fervice in the weftern parts, I was fo perfectly tired with the drudgery of it, that I demanded as a right (by vertue of that ordinance) to have leave to deliver up my charge; which, I thank God, I performed without any difturbance or diforder. I

I am

I am led into this impertinency only to let the world know I was never either a fouldier or courtier of fortune: and, therefore (if an argument from a probability may be admitted), not fo likely, either out of neceffity, or ambition, to have ends upon a new warr.

But the queftion will not be, what good thoughts or inclinations I have formerly had (for that may feem to make no more for my juftification, then the having had a good dream), nor how willingly and contentedly I quitted my employment (for that may be interpreted by fome as an act of paffion; or, at the beft, of no merit: I did but what I ought to have done). But the iffue will be, what my actions are and have been, in reference to the following troubles. To clear that I muft be enforced to look back again, as farr as to the conclufion of the above mentioned laft report from Saffron Waldon, and to refume that narrative of the paffages between the army and

and Parliament; whereby, I hope, I shall make it appear evidently, that the Parliament was necessitated to put on a posture of defence against the treacherous and insidious attempts of the army (I mean the party that acted it), and that I did nothing but by order, and in order to that defence. So that there can ly no crime against me, but that I was obedient and subservient to the Parliament; of which, if I had not been guilty, it had been a crime. I shall do this briefly, and in a coasting way, not troubling myself to put into every little creek; but observing only the principal capes and inletts of this fatal difference.

The Parliament having taken the report aforesaid (made by Sir John Clotworthy and myself) into consideration, and signify'd their acceptation of our poor endeavours to do them service, was much divided, with the sense of those divisions in the army, between joy and grief. They could not but fett their hearts (with joy)

upon

upon those officers and souldiers that had declared themselves willing to hazard their lives, in the high places of the field, against the rebels of Ireland; in demonstration whereof, they immediately passed whatsoever we had offered for their encouragement. On the other side, they were not without great thoughts of heart, for the divisions of those that would neither stirr abroad, nor be still at home. To reclaim their restiness, many things were proposed in a special manner; care was taken to give them satisfaction in the point of arrears and indemnity; and touching the last, there was an ordinance passed with further enlargements.

But whilest this was *sub incude,* and not yet thorowly hammered, the House received advertisement, that the army began to be haunted with apparitions, certain spirits, and dominations, conjur'd up out of the body of the souldiery, under the title of agitators; things never known before, in any

any army in the world, and now set up, in confutation of Ecclesiastes, to shew, that there might be a novelty under the sun. Their employment was for two ends, the one, to engage the common souldiers in the designe of the officers, and to incorporate all in one and the same interest; the other, to put on those desperate attempts, and, as wedges, to make way through those knots, where the great officers did not think fitt to hazard their own finer hedges and points. The advantage of this was, that if any thing succeeded not, it was discharg'd upon the passion and wildness of the souldiers: if it took effect, those who were behind the curteine, and acted those puppets, had opportunity to improve all to their own ends. The first publick notice that the Parliament had given them of this invention (for it may be reckon'd among Pancirollus his *nova reperta),* was upon the occasion of two letters, both dated the 30th of April, 1647, and signed by the agitators of eight regiments of horse, the one addressed to the Field Marshall Skippon, the other to Lieutenant Generall Cromwell, and by them communicated to the House. They were both but the same in substance, *mutatis mutandis,* conteining a complaint of some foxes (and I know not what kind of vermine) supposed to be protected by those who were intrusted with the government of the kingdome, and who having lately tasted of sovereinety, were degenerated into tyrants. They protested against the service of Ireland, and all persons that had engaged in it; and plainly declared, that whosoever should go in that command, (though never so faithfull) they must shew themselvs averse, untill their desires were granted, and (which was then a new style), the just rights and liberties of the subjects of England vindicated and mainteined.

To give a stop unto these beginnings of strife, which otherwise, like a breach of waters,

waters, threatned to make way through all sluces and bounds; it was resolved, That the Field Marshall Skippon, Lieutenant Generall Cromwell, Commissary Generall Ireton, and Colonel Fleetwood, should be sent down to Saffron Walden, where the head-quarters were still continued, with instructions to communicate the aforesaid votes concerning arrears, and the ordinance of indemnity to the army; and to use their best endeavours to allay distempers, and to beget a clear understanding between the army and the Parliament. At the first convention of the officers, there was little done, more than in a preparatory way to the next meeting, a question demanded by some of them, What was meant by the word Distempers? and answered (like Sisera's mother) by themselvs, that if it signify'd grievances, they had then matter enough to offer. But yet, in regard it might seem a precipitate and irregular act in them, to undertake to declare the sense

May the 7th, 1647.

of

of the army, before they had confulted with it, they defired time for that, and for to make their report upon it, until the 14th of May following. This was clearly but fo much time loft, as to the bufinefs. For they confefs'd themfelvs they had the ftuff already by them, and might as well have cutt it out then as afterwards, if it had fo pleafed them. But it was for their credit that they fhould feem not to lead, but to be driven, and put on by others, upon thofe reprefentations. And befides, in the gain of fo many days they had a good advantage to chafe, and heat the army thoroughly, to make it the more ductile, and pliant to further impreffions.

At the next returne, when divers of the officers were ready to prefent the condition of the forces, under their refpective commands, in a fair and open way, according to their former orders from the Comfioners; it pleafed Colonel Lambert, and fom others, to interpofe, upon a pretence that

that they were entrufted to draw up, and authorized to reprefent the grievances of the whole army; which being utterly difclaimed by thofe gentlemen (as a thing without their privity, or any commiffion at all) the debate grew fo high, that affronts pafs'd between them, and there was a cry to withdraw, which if it had taken effect, would have produced a bloody iffue among them. This proceeding drew on that diffent, and proteftation of an hundred fixty-seven officers, wherein they defired, that Colonel Lambert, and the reft of thofe pretended plenipotentiaries with him, might be made to fhew what warrant they had to ingrofs into their hands the returns fent in from the feveral regiments, troops, or companies of the army; or what authority to vary in a fyllable from the fenfe of thofe that employ'd them; and preffed, that thofe particular returns might be delivered in to the Commiffioners, and attefted before them, to the end they might be clearly and infallibly

Vindicat. of 167 officers.

infallibly informed of the true temper of the army, in every part thereof. The Field Marſhal at the firſt carried himſelf in an equitable way, and declared his opinion upon the place, that nothing could paſs as the general ſenſe of the army, ſo long as there was ſuch a diſſenting party. But yet, nevertheleſs, afterward coming to a Pilate temper, when he ſaw that he avayled nothing; but that more tumult was made, he gave way to the impetuoſity of Colonel Lambert, and that party; and proceeded to take their repreſentative bill of complaint into conſideration.

The firſt ſtone of offence that was ſtumbled at was, the declaration of the Houſes againſt the petition; which, they ſaid, was but an application to their Generall for relief, in things meerly concerning them, as ſouldiers, and no way condemnable. The next exception was at a report, that they ſhould invite the King to come unto them, with a promiſe to ſet the crown upon his

his head, which was interpreted then as a great scandal. And lastly, it was ill taken, that it should be said they had received fower thousand of the King's souldiers into their army; whereas, among five and twenty thousand horse and foot, they had but one commissioned officer that had served on that side, and he came recommended unto them, by an authority derived from the Parliament.

I shall say nothing to their demands as souldiers, in reference to the petition; but that their following actions have given sufficient demonstration, how well they have kept themselves within the circle of that duty. As for their exception to that report, concerning the King, by their good leave, it carried some probability of a truth with it. For they might as well have invited him then, as they soon after compelled him to come to their feast, which (after the manner of the Jews) was accompany'd with a sacrifice, wherein his own royal perfon prov'd to be the oblation. What crowns and fceptres they promifed him Lieutenant Colonel Lillburne and Major Huntington have fufficiently fhewn. For the point of that recruit out of the King's forces, poffibly they may have been wronged in the account of fower thoufand cavaliers, faid to have been taken on by them: though fome have reported, there were no lefs than five thoufand. But all that I fhall take notice of in that kinde is, that when my Lord of Warwick, and the reft of us were at Waldon, upon the forementioned employment, we had certain information given us by a grave minifter, that in one poor country village in Suffolk, upon the edge of Cambridgefhire (the place where he himfelf lived), of twenty fouldiers which were quartered there, there were no lefs then nineteen that had been in actual fervice againft the Parliament. And for that plea, that they had but one commiffioned officer in the army, that had been

been on the King's fide, it doth not alter the cafe, but that with the allowance of nine hundred ninety-nine fouldiers, the difference may be reconciled. But who ever had wrong, I am fure the ftate had no right, in the mufter roll of five and twenty thoufand horfe and foot, which were more by fower thoufand then were allowed by the eftablifhment, and thofe taken on when the warr was at an end (without the confent or knowledge of the Houfes). It feems there was an end beyond that end.

The Field Marfhall having thus (contrary to all reafon and confcience) given entertainment to thofe caufelefs complaints, put a clofure to this meeting, with the publication of his intention to go for Ireland, and defired the officers to acquaint the fouldiers with it, and to let them know what votes the Houfes had pafs'd for their encouragement. At the third convention, the report was that both the
votes

votes and the resolution of the Field Marshall had been communicated to the army; whereupon the souldiers had chosen a Committee of members selected out of every troop and company of the army, which being assembled at St. Edmundsbury in Suffolk, had resolved upon the question certain grievances, and transmitted them to the officers. That the officers, upon perusal of them, had put themselvs into a grand committee, and digested those scattered returns into one orderly forme, which they besought the Field Marshal to present to the Parliament, as the common sense of the whole army. The reason of their single application to him was, because Lieutenant Generall Cromwell, and the rest of the Commissioners, refused to appear in the business, as being persons interested in, and relating to the army.

The result of all was, that distemper in the army, there was none, as to that, *omnia bene*: But the grievances were these: First, that

that they had not a conftant pay, to difcharge quarters, whereby they were render'd burthenfome and odious to the people.
Secondly, that there was no courfe taken
that they might have their debenturs before they were difbanded. Thirdly, that
the act of indemnity (though fo often tried,
and purified), was not yet perfected, as it
fhould be. Fourthly, that they were de-
barred from petitioning, contrary to that
right which was due unto them, both as
fouldiers and Englifhmen. Fifthly, they
demanded a revocation of the ordinance
againft the petition. Laftly, a reparation
to be made for the commitment of Enfigne
Nichols, a member of the army.

Thefe were the particulars, wherein the
army, as a Parliament, required fatisfaction
of the Parliament; of all which the Field
Marfhal gave a fpeedy account to the Houfe,
with an intimation, that he found the bufinefs harfh, and rugged, and in importance

of

of it, exceeding all that he had yet met with. Upon this return, it was thought fitt, and refolved, that the Generall fhould be defired to repair forthwith unto the army, to keep it the better in order; and that a letter fhould be written to the Commiffioners, to fend up any one, or two of their number, to make report of their proceedings; the Field Marfhal only excepted, who was ordered to ftay there, for the better advancing of the fervice for Ireland, and to take off the fouldiers, from halting between two employments (whereby their humors were kept ftirring, and working), and to make them fettle upon a refolution either to go for Ireland, or to fit down quietly at home with a difcharge: it was voted, that all the forces of the kingdome, not fubfcribing for the fervice of Ireland, fhould be difbanded (excepting thofe formerly ordered to be kept up for the maintenance of fuch garrifons as were to be continued); and

and that it should be referred to the Committee of Darby House, to consider of the time, and manner of disbanding them.

May the 21st the General took his journey to Walden, and our commissioners (all but the Field Marshal), returned to London. The same day, the Houses (that they might shew their preventing grace), before the report was made, passed the act of indemnity, as fully and amply as could be in conscience desired, or in justice devised. Upon the report (which was but the same, flourished into larger expressions, with what I have delivered in few words, and as it were wound up in the bottom), they proceeded to these votes. First, that the souldiers arrears should be speedily audited, and a visible security given them for so much of their arrears, as should not be paid off upon disbanding. Secondly, that an ordinance should be drawn up, to make good the declaration of both Houses for apprentices of London, and other corporations,

tions, to have their time allowed them, that had ſerved in the warr for the Parliament. Thirdly, that there ſhould be an ordinance, to exempt all ſuch as had voluntarily ſerved as ſouldiers under the Parliament, from being preſſed to any forreign ſervice. And fourthly, that an ordinance ſhould be paſſed, for providing ſufficient maintenance for widows, and maimed ſouldiers, and orphans in all the counties of the kingdome. All the propoſitions of the army being thus anſwered, the Houſes reſolved to go through with their work, and not to make an end before they had don. In order whereunto, they immediately apply'd themſelves to the raiſing of moneys; which was indeed the right way; and without which all their votes, and orders, and ordinances, would have ſignified very little, or nothing.

In the mean time, the Committee at Darby-houſe went to work, as they were appointed by the above-mentioned vote, to ſettle

settle the manner of disbanding; and (not thinking it a business fit to be kept cold) without further delay. May the 25th made report, that the General's regiment of foot, as neerest in quarters, and first in order, should begin the example; their rendezvous to be at Chelmsford in Essex; where so many of them as would engage for Ireland, should be presently taken on, and have a fortnight's pay advanced to them out of their six week's pay, besides the two months of their arrears, with direction to march to Ingerstone, where they should receive further orders. Those that would disband, upon the delivering up their arms, to have two month's pay allowed them, and passes to their homes. The like method to be respectively held with all the regiments in the army, both horse and foot (excepting those reserved upon the new establishment), the money's to discharge all this, ordered to be conveyed at the same time, to the several places of rendezvous.

To

To actuate these orders, the Earl of Warwick, the Lord de la Ware, Sir Gilbert Gerard, Sir John Potts, Mr. Grimstone, and Mr. Knightly were appointed Commissioners by the Houses, with instructions, to assist Sir Thomas Fairfax in the disbanding, and to publish in the head of every regiment (together with the votes lately passed), a declaration from the Parliament, in acknowledgment of their gallant and faithfull service, and to assure them, that there was no ill talent lodged towards them for any thing passed. This civility was at the same time realized, in the discharge of Ensign Nichols, and other officers of the army, who stood accused of misdemeanours of a very high nature.

The Generall, upon these advertisements, being extremely surprised, and at a loss, not knowing what to do, seeing things brought to so neer a birth, called a council of warr the same night that he received the intelligence, and with such privado's

as

as he had about him, takes a suddain resolution to remove his head quarters from Walden to St. Edmund's Bury in Suffolk, and gave order to all the officers to meet him there, and to his own regiment to follow him thither; (a way, clean contrary from the place assigned for the disbanding thereof). At this convention, for want of better employment, they voted down the votes of the Houses, as unsatisfactory; and resolved to contract their quarters, in order to a general rendezvous, for a march; and to engage the army, they demanded a right against those persons, that had intended, and complotted to break it; (which is, by interpretation, to disband it according to the ordinance of Parliament). This came to the House, by a letter from the Generall, bearing date from St. Edmund's Bury, the 30th of May 1647; about which time the Earle of Warwick, and the rest of the Commissioners with him, certify'd to how little purpose they

remained

remained at Chelmsford, luring after a regiment that had taken flight as far as Bury. Whereupon it was ordered, that both they and the Field Marſhal (whoſe negotiation had been as fruitleſs, as their journey to no end) ſhould be recalled, and the money ſent for the diſbanding, returned. Thoſe ſumms, that were carried to Chelmſford, had the great good fortune to finde the way home again, but all that was ſent to Oxford, notwithſtanding the protection of the Parliament, was arreſted by the ſouldiers.

Theſe proceedings put the Houſe into great perplexity: for remedy whereof divers expedients were offered; ſome were for vigorous counſails, as in ſuch a caſe, not only the moſt honourable, but the moſt ſafe; others were of different opinions, according to their ſeveral complexions, or intereſts. But the Field Marſhal, being then preſent, was look'd upon by moſt, as likelyeſt to fitt an advice, ſuitable to the conſtitution of the army, who had ſo lately taken

taken the meafure of it. He thereupon (with a great deal of gravity) making report of all the forementioned paffages, in the conclufion deliver'd his judgment, that it would be beft, to follow moderate counfails, and to comply with the prefent paffion of the fouldiers, which, having open way given to it, might poffibly fpend itfelf; but, being obftructed, would fwell and rife higher, to the ruine of all that lay before it. This coming from a perfon fo knowing, and fo known, in an unhappy hour, fway'd the Houfe; though not without a prognofticating apprehenfion in many, that in handling thefe nettles fo gently, we fhould but fting our own fingers in the end.

In purfuance of this advice, it was refolved, Firft, that an ordinance fhould be brought in, to authorize, and make good in law, the affignment of debentures, and to give protection to fuch officers, as were attending upon committees of accounts, that they might not be lyable to arrests for debt, during the time of that attendance; provided it did not exceed two months. Secondly, that such officers, as were in prison, should have their accounts first audited; and their arrears first paid. Thirdly, that such officers, as could not attend the perfecting of their accounts, should leave them in the hands of the committee, the House declaring, that they would do with them, in their absence, as they would do with others in that case. Fourthly, that the committee should perfect, and dispatch the accounts of the officers of the kingdom, and returne them to the House, so soon as they were perfected. Fifthly, that the common souldiers should have all their arrears, deducting for free quarters, according to the ordinary rates of the army. Sixthly, that the subordinate officers, not in commission, should have the like. Seventhly, that the commissionate officers of the army should have one month's pay more,

more, added to the two month's pay formerly voted. Eighthly, that a letter should be written to the Generall to give him an account, what the house had don, in satisfaction to the army, desiring him to contine his care to preserve the army in order, and under discipline, that there might be no disturbance. Ninthly, there was ten thousand pounds ordered, to satisfy the present necessity of the officers, and souldiers, whose accounts were either stated, or stating, to be advanced upon the credit of the moitie of the compositions at Goldsmith's Hall, and payed to the committees, where Colonel Birch, and Mr. Goodwin, had the chair, to be by them distributed in such proportions, as those two committees (who were joyned as to that business) should think fitt. And lastly, that the declaration against the petition should be razed out of the journals of the Houses; which was accordingly performed in both to the huge diminution of the honour of them both.

And now the parliament might have put the queſtion, *Quid faciendum amplius?* What more could have been don for the army, that was not don? There was nothing of difference left, except (like the teſty *Ælius*, they would have been angry, becauſe they had no cauſe to be angry. But this overflowing grace, which ſhould have meliorated, and improved them, and have made them yield fruits worthy of amendment, did (like the Nilus, when it riſeth too high) breed a ſterility, and make thoſe degenerate plants unproductive of any thing, but the wilde grapes of rebellion, and diſobedience. For inſteed of being led to repentance by this goodneſs, they grew wanton and inſolent upon it, interpreting all theſe conceſſions, but as ſo many demonſtrations of fear and puſillanimity; and thereupon took new courage,

Iſai. v. 4.

Sen. de ira l. 3. c. 8.

and

and refolved to follow their point. And whilft the Houfes, for their further fatiffaction were bufied in paffing the ordinance of indemnity again, with new additions (as if they had thought, that nothing but too much, could be enough for them), they were as bufily employ'd in carrying on their mines, and laying their trains, to blow up the Houfes. 4 Jun. 1647.

I muft ftill repeat my defire, to be clearly underftood, that I fpeak not in this of the whole body of the army, without diftinction, or regard of perfons; but only in reference to the fuperior officers, and their party; who, doubting how farr thofe condefcentions might operate upon the fouldiers, and not confident of their ftrength in the Houfe of Commons, and the city, took a bold refolution, to feife upon the perfon of the King at Holdenby; that where their fox-furr would not hold out, they might be able to piece it out with the lion's fkin; whereby upon occafion, only to make ufe of his Majefty's abfent prefence (like Alexander's empty chair) to give countenance to their proceedings; but likewife to ingratiate themfelvs, both with his party, by feeding them with airy hopes (the pooreft diet in the world), that they would reftore him to his crown and dignity; and with the city, by putting them into an expectation that they would bring him unto his Parliament, whereby their trade and cuftome would be revived again: fo becoming all things to all to gain their own ends.

This egg was laid, in Lieutenant Generall Cromwell's own chamber, and brooded between him, and Commiffary Generall Ireton; but they were too wife to cackle; *Quod movet, quiefcit.* Cornet Joyce was employ'd, as the man to hatch it; who, having receiv'd his orders from the Lieutenant Generall, firft to make fure of the garrifon at Oxford, and the gunns and ammunition there; and then to march to

Holdenby,

Holdenby, in purfuance of the former advice, did (like a man of his trade) go through ftitch with his bufinefs. To lay a fmooth oyl upon the face of this treafon, there was a neceffity pretended in it, that it was to anticipate and prevent a plott, faid to be contrived by a malignant party in the Houfe of Commons, whereby the King fhould have been remov'd from Holdenby, either to fome place of ftrength, or into the head of another army, or brought up to London, by Colonel Graves, by the advice of the commiffioners there, who, for fo doing, would have adventured to caft themfelvs upon the favourable conftruction of the Parliament. All this was mere fiction and poetry, but it ferved their turne well enough for the prefent, who were fo confcientious, that rather then fuch a wicked act (as to feife upon the King) fhould be done by others, they would do it themfelvs.

Of this force his Majefty gave advertifement,

tisement to both the Houses, by the Earl of Dunfermlin; which was received with a sad astonishment, and not without a prognostication of those fatal effects which have since ensued. In the mean time, the Generall, and superior officers, disclaimed those villanous proceedings, and washed their hands in innocency, and none but the mad-headed souldier bore the blame. So among the Athenians, when a sacrifice was slain, the priests and assistants were free from the blood of it, and nothing found guilty but the sword that did the execution. For the Generall (who was but too innocent), I am clearly of opinion that he was a stranger to this designe. For when Joyce his letter came to him at Keinton, acquainting him with the removal of the King, and letting him know that he was upon his march with him towards Newmarket, he was displeased at it, and told the Commissary Generall Ireton, that he did not like it, demanding who gave those orders

Ælian. Var. Hist. l. viii. c. 2.

orders; and the Commiffary acknowledged, that he gave them; but it was only for fecuring the King there, and not for the taking him away from thence. But the Lieutenant Generall coming then from London (from whence he was fecretly ftol'n, after he had publickly, in the Houfe of Commons, difclaimed all intelligence with the army, as to their mutinous proceedings, and invoked the curfe of GOD upon himfelf, and his pofterity, if ever he fhould joyne, or combine with them, in any actings or attempts contrary to the orders of the Houfe), he owned the bufinefs, and that was enough to ftop his mouth. The fame day, Cornet Joyce being told, that the Generall was difpleafed with him for bringing the King from Holdenby, anfwered, that Lieutenant Generall Cromwell gave him order at London for all that he had don, either there or at Oxford.

But once, whether the woman did it, or the

the serpent, however it fell out, neither the Generall, nor his officers, would be so uncivil, as to offer to undo what others had done. They were, by no means, consenting to the felony; but yet very willing to receive the purchase; and resolute to keep it too, notwithstanding the demand of the Parliament to the contrary. For evidence of this, the Generall himself, in his letter to the House of Commons, undertook to be the keeper of his Majesty's head, to preserve him from danger, and to prevent any mischief that might fall out by a new warr (a new word, then minted, but afterward of great use), protesting, both for himself and the army, that they had no other desire, then to see a firme peace settled, and the liberty of the people vindicated and cleared: and if they might meet with a publick concurrence in these things, it would be a great encouragement to a cheerfull, and unanimous disbanding. The close of all was, an assurance that whatever
might

might be suggested or suspected, the army was neither opposite to the Presbyterian, nor partial to the Independent, nor fond of a licencious government, for the advantage of parties or interests; but left all to the wisdome of the House.

The Parliament was now (if I may speak it with reverence) somthing in the condition of Balaam, intranced with their eyes open: they saw, with a sad astonishment, that all their retractions and compliances had served to no other end, but to give the souldiers knowledge of their weakness; and that this knowledge (instead of a better edification) had but puff'd them up in their demands, and given them the presumption to put the sword into the scales, with a *Quid nisi dolor victis?* In those perplexities, as in troubled waters, the more we stirr, the less we see, Numb. xxiv. 4.

——————*Obscuraq moto*
Reddita forma lacu est.

The more the Houses troubled themselvs with thinking, the less they knew what to think. But it was truly said, Once out, and ever out. *Semel turbatis confiliis, multi deinceps sequuntur errores.* They had been already diverted out of the way of honour by dough-bak'd counsails, and now they were engaged in a low way (which is commonly the dirtiest) they must plunge through it as well as they could. To help themselvs out of the mire, they agree to send new commissioners to addulce, and sweeten the army, and to charme it, as much as might be, into the circle of obedience. The persons employ'd were the Earle of Nottingham, the Lord de la Ware, Sir Henry Vane the younger, the Field Marshal Skippon, Mr. Scawen, and Mr. Pory; (some of these intimate cabalists with the superior officers of the army). Their instructions were to publish the forementioned votes in the head of the army, and
to

to perfuade difbanding; this to be done at a general rendezvous appointed upon Newmarket Heath.

But before they could come thither, the army (upon this intelligence) had faved them fo much labour, and was advanced to a rendezvous at Triplo, five miles from Cambridge, and nearer London, towards which they now began to caft a fquinting eye. By the way, at Cambridge, they kept a faft, *ad contentionem & jurgium*. Is it fuch a faft that GOD hath chofen? Is it not rather *jejunium Diabolicum*, to faft from meat (the devils eat nothing) to ruminate on mifchief? Can there be a greater wickednefs, then to make GOD an acceffary to wickednefs, as if he were fuch a one as themfelves? But the Commiffioners from the Parliament mett them there, and faw their pious impieties; and they had their reward. The next day the army was drawn up in a large meadow ground, within four miles of Royfton; where the

Ifai. viii. 4. 5.

Pfal. l. 21

votes

votes were publickly read, and seconded by the Field Marshal with a short speech, to make them go down the better. Answer was made by an officer of the Generall's regiment of horse, that it was desired they might have liberty to peruse the votes, and return their sense by some of the officers and agitators deputed to that purpose; whereunto some of the souldiers, to signify their concurrence, acclaimed, All, All; and after (according to their lesson), Justice, Justice! And this was the no-end of that day's work, the army from thence marching to their quarters in and about Royston.

Upon this advance the city of London began to take alarm, and to fret at the voisinage of such a distemper'd multitude, likely (besides other mischiefs) to lick up all provisions round about them, as an oxe licketh up the grass of the field; which unto so vast a populacy, so divided in itself, and in a dead time of trade, was extremely considerable.

confiderable. To prevent all inconveniencies, it was ordered by the Houfes upon a petition from the city, that the army fhould approch no nearer to London then fourty miles; and letters were directed to the Generall, to that effect. But whilft thefe things were under deliberation, the Generall had difpach'd up a fummons to the city, (it was no other in effect), dated from Royfton, the 10th of June 1647, and figned by himfelf, and twelve field officers; wherein they reprefented themfelvs under a double notion, as fouldiers and as Englifhmen; as fouldiers, they confeffed they were limited to their former demands; but as Englifhmen, they claimed a further latitude to inquire into the government of the ftate, and the liberties of the fubject (as if the Parliament had been out of office, and not habilitated to take cognifance of fuch matters. This diftinction was never coined by Scotus nor Aquinas; but ow's itfelf to Lieutenant Generall Cromwell, who made

L good

good use of it to the agitators, as an engine to screw them up to heighten their demands, and who offer'd it to the King as a ground of persuasion, to induce him to hearken to the desires of the army, and to entertein a treaty with them upon their proposals. But by the way, it puts me in mind of a story of a country fellow in Germany, who seing the Lord of the town where he lived, shew himself in the field, in arms, in the morning, and in the church in his pontificals in the evening, demanded the reason, and being told that it was to signify his double capacity, the one as a temporal lord, the other as an ecclesiastick or churchman, he desired to know whether the ecclesiastic could be a saint, when the temporal lord was a devil; and whether in one capacity he could find the way to Heaven, when he should be sent to hell in the other. I do not know, but a man might have ask'd those Gentlemen, that profess'd themselvs souldiers and Englishmen, and made themselvs felvs lords and churchmen, whether the Englishman can preserve his honour, when the souldier hath forfeited his faith? Whether the Englishman can avow the usurpation of mastership over the Parliament, when the souldier is a servant to it? As to the fortune of those gentlemen in the next world, who held this opinion, I say nothing but that it is well if they come to have good quarters there.

But to go on with the letter. They made great professions, that they desired to alter nothing in the civil government, nor to interrupt the settlement of the Presbyterian discipline, nor to open a way to any unbridled liberty of conscience; though they could wish that every man of a peaceable and blameless conversation, and that were beneficial to the commonwealth, might have liberty and encouragement. (which is no other in plain English, but that any man might hold any opinion, though never so impious, as long as he used a good trade, and kept the peace: by which rule the church would come to be governed, like Fryer John's Colledge in Rabelias, by one general statute, Do what you list.

———— *Ridente dicere verum.*
Quid vetat?

Those, they said, were their modest desires, for the obteining whereof they were drawing near the city, without any intention to do hurt to it, and rather then any evil should befall it, they would be their bulwark, and the souldiers should make their way through their blood. The conclusion was a flat menace of ruine, and destruction, if they should offer to take up arms in opposition to, or hindrance of those their just undertakings.

This letter being presented to the Parliament by the citizens, was insteed of a reveille, to rouze them up to look about them, and to prepare for action, letting them plainly see there was nothing to be gained

gained by stooping to the army, but to be trampled under foot by it; and that now they must resolve either to do, or suffer. Whereupon, that they might be in a fitting posture, either to repell force with force; or otherwise to fall, like that Roman senate, with honour, and to sett clear in their lowest condition, they ordered, that there should be a Committee of Safety appointed to be joyned with the citizens, for advice concerning their common preservation. They ordered some forces to be raised; and things were putting into an handsome preparation.

11° Junii, 1647.

But the army partly in the city, foreseeing how ruinous, and destructive, the prosecution of this way would be, to the carrying on of their designe, immediately interposed, upon fair and specious pretences of preventing misunderstandings, and saving of further effusion of bloud; and so farr prevailed in the Common Council, that they persuaded them, to return a soft, and gentle

gentle anfwer (with the approbation of the Parliament) unto the aforefaid letter; and engaged them to fupplicate the Houfes, that they would take into their fpeedy confideration, the juft defires of the army, and apply fuch remedies unto them, as fhould be thought fitt. They likewife obtained, that Alderman Fowke, Alderman Gibbs, and fome others joyned with them, fhould repaire with all expedition to the army (as commiffioners from the city) to prefent their anfwer to the Generall; and to give, and receive fuch further fatisfaction, concerning the matter conteined therein, as occafion fhould require. The fcope of the anfwer was this; that they acknowledged, the former good fervices of the army, and thanked them for their profeffion, not to act any thing to the prejudice, either of the Parliament, or city. But yet, neverthelefs, in regard this approach might of itfelf give occafion, to increafe the price of victuall, and give opportunity

portunity to difcontented perfons, to raife tumults, and diforders; they defired the army would forbear quartering, within thirty miles of the city. They protefted againft all thoughts of levying a new warr; and declared, that that pofture of defence, whereinto they had putt themfelvs, by direction of the Parliament, was not in oppofition to, or hindrance of the juft defires of the army; (which they had recommended in their humble addrefs to the Houfes), but only to defend the Parliament, and themfelvs, againft any unlawfull violence; appealing to GOD, and to the prefent and future generations to judge between them.

This letter, and the defires of the citizens, were offer'd to the Parliament by Alderman Fowke, and were affented to 12° Junii, 1647. The Houfe not thinking it fitt to conteft with thofe, by whome (as the cafe then ftood), they were to subfift. If the foundations fail, what can the best men do? But hereby the party of the army received an huge encouragement, and indeed gained their end; which was no other, then to retard, and flacken their preparations for defence. There is nothing so mortall to active counsells, as to suffer them to take cold in their birth. To speak a sad truth, the destruction of the Parliament was from itself, by an equal failer in their proceedings, both at the first, when they began to question the officers, and in the close of this unhappy businefs, when they began to put themselvs into a defensive posture. For, if either they had gone roundly to work with these gentlemen, when they had them at the barr before them, to dispose of them as they pleased, they had crushed the cockatrice in the egg; or if now they had gon through with their resolution, to maintein their honour with their swords in their hands, and had declared in a gallant free way against those rebellious practises, and actings, that

that would have infallibly ftrengthened the hands of the citizens, and reformados; and rendred all the fulminations of the army brutifh, and infignificant. Either way, they might have given fufficient demonftration of their vertue and courage; which, in the true nature of it, fhould be (according to that riddle of the fhadow in Athenæus) *in ortu, & interitu maxima,* in the rifing, and fetting of dangers moft confpicuous. But the Houfes, by this unfeafonable tendernes, and refervation, keeping themfelvs upon a faluting pofture, when they could have prefented, and been ready to give fire, cooled the metall of thofe that were beft affected to their fervice, with a juft doubt, in what way to act againft thofe as enemies, who (for ought they yet knew) might be owned as friends; and at laft, they brought that dampe upon themfelvs, that putt out the light in their own counfells. When the light went out, Leander drowned.

<small>Athen. Dipnos, l. 10. c. 19.</small>

<small>Mufeus.</small>

All

All this while there was not one word returned from the army, in anfwer to the letters and votes publifhed at Triplo Heath. It feems, the fons of Anak looked upon the poor Lords and Commons but as fo many grafhoppers fitted to be walked over, then regarded. Their anfwer was, an advance; and then, the Generall took the pains to certify the Houfes, that (very unluckily), before the receipt of their letters, forbidding him to approche nearer then fourty miles unto the city, he was engaged upon his march to St. Albans, and could not handfomely face about; but he doubted not to give a good account of his actions. In the mean time, a month's pay (the wages of unrighteoufnefs), was defired to be fent fpeedily to the army, that they might not be burthenfome to the country, by taking free-quarter, with a kinde promife not to draw nearer then twenty miles to London, without firft giving the Parliament notice thereof. This was a pure
fcoine

scorne. There is nothing more miserable in misery. *Quam quod ridiculos homines facit.* But the bramble was now grown so high, that a fire must consume the cedars of Lebanon, if they would not put themselves under his umbrage. To countenance these excentrick and irregular motions, there were, about this time, several petitions tendred to the Generall (the copies whereof were sent up to the Houses by the Commissioners), which desired the army might not disband, until the public grievances of the kingdom were redressed, justice executed, and peace settled. They were reported to come from the counties of Essex, Northfolk, and Suffolk, but known to be framed in the army, and were attested only by a few inconsiderable hands privatly gained by the brokerage of som independent factors; and so they edified little, and caught none but those that were in the trapp before. That which most perplexed the Parliament, was, the uncertainty (after

all

all thofe hoverings) where the army would fix, and upon what demands they would finally infift. To found this, Sir Thomas Widrington, and Colonel White, were fent to the Quarters, as additional Commiffioners, with inftructions to ufe the beft ways and means they could, to difcover what their particular defignes were, and what would at laft give them a full fatisfaction.

In the mean time, the Houfes had notice of intentions of putting the king into the head of the army; not for his fafety, freedome, or honour, but only to make him a ftale, to deceive people with and to facilitate their reception into the city. Whereupon to prevent all inconveniencies, and (if poffible) to free his royal perfon out of their pawes, who plaid with him only with an intent to devour him at laft, there was an order fent of the 15th of June, 1647, to require the Generall to deliver his Majefty unto the Commiffioners formerly appointed to receive him at Newcaftle, or to any

any three of them, who ſhould conduct him to Richmond, and attend him there, under the gard of Colonel Roſſiter, with his regiment, whereby alſo (beſides that moſt important conſideration of his ſecurity) the Houſes might be in a better capacity, at ſo near a diſtance, to preſent their humble addreſſes unto him, in order to a ſpeedy ſettlement of affairs. But the officers of the army had provided aforehand againſt this trick (like good gameſters that conſider what cards are againſt them, and accordingly play their own game), for they had been importunate with the King, to procure his conſent to ſtay with them, engaging their bodies and ſouls to do him ſervice; and finding his averſneſs from them, and his determination to cloſe (if poſſibly he could) with the Parliament; and being eſpecially moved with that expreſſion of his, that he would go to receive the addreſſes of his two Houſes, according to their invitation of him;

him; and if any fhould prefume to lay hold upon his bridle to ftop him, he would endeavour to make it his laft; to make all fure, they kept continual gards upon him, as if, according to that expreffion of Antigonus, concerning the guarding of Eumenes, he had been a lion or an elephant; and to prevent any attempt that might be made to refcue him, they kept likewife good out-guards; fo fecuring him, that they needed not to fear the lofing of him, or his being taken from them. And this ftrictnefs was continued, untill the coming down of the forementioned votes, fignifying the compliance of the Parliament with the defires of the army: for then, and never till then his Majefty began to incline an ear to the follicitations of Lieutenant Generall Cromwell, and Commiffary Generall Ireton; whereupon there was a fair refpect put on towards him, as to a perfon now likely to be gained to their party.

Æmil. Prob. in Eumene.

In this conjuncture, to amufe the Houfes, and

and to give them other business to think on, there was sent up a letter accompany'd with a declaration, of the 15th of June, from the army, boldly requiring, First, that the House of Commons might be speedily purged of such as ought not to sitt there. Secondly, that such persons as abused the Parliament and army, and endangered the kingdome might be speedily disabled. Thirdly, that a sett time might be limited, for the determination of the present Parliament, and for the beginning, and ending of future Parliaments. Fourthly, that there might be a free liberty to the subject to petition the parliament, when they could have no other remedy. Fifthly, that all arbitrary powers of Committees, or Deputy Lieutenants, might cease, and be abrogate. Sixthly, that the kingdome might be satisfy'd in point of accounts. Lastly, that an act of oblivion might be passed. The duplicate of this declaration was brought to the city, by the

the hands of their Commissioners, together with a complimental letter to assure them of the good affections of the army, provided that they would be quiet, and not offer to intermeddle. *In transitu*, I cannot but reflect upon these propositions; of which the third, concerning the determination both of this, and of future Parliaments, and the fifth, for the abrogation of the arbitrary power of Committees, &c. had been formerly moved in the House of Commons, by the Presbyterian Party, and rejected by the Independents; and yet were now in (a jesuitical way) obtruded by the army, as agreable to the sense of the Independents, to be passed as their act; that they might turn the envy of those burthens, and pressures upon the Presbyterians, and ingratiate themselvs with the kingdom at their expense. Whether there were not more of the serpent, then of the dove in this, let GOD and the world judge. The fourth, about liberty of petitioning, was

never

never denyed. None but that Sicilian tyrant could delight, rather to hear the bellowings, then to underſtand the grievances of poor people. It is a wanton cruelty to make men cry, and not ſuffer them to ſpeak. The Houſes did never yet ſhutt their doors againſt petitioners, that made their addreſſes to them in an orderly way. But when ſouldiers in an army ſhall be engaged by ſom of their Officers, in a petition, by perſonal ſubſcription, which, *in naturâ rei*, is no other then a combination to a mutiny; and when ſome inconſiderable perſons in a city ſhall preſume to offer petitions in the name of the city, without the privity or conſent of the Common Council (which is a meer cheatt put upon the government), it could not but be neceſſary, to lay a regulation upon that liberty. The reſt of the propoſitions were ſuch, as either had already been anſwered (if a ſatisfaction could have given a ſatisfaction), or were at that time under deliberation,

deliberation, and therefore I pass them by, and proceed to the return of the City Commissioners, and the account of their stewardship.

Those gentlemen, or some of them, acted their parts so well, and charmed the Common Council and Militia so wisely, that they persuaded them, the army was compounded, and elemented of nothing, but goodness and integrity; and that it would be a sin, to lead them into temptation, by provoking and imitating them with any hostile preparations; and thereupon obteined, to have all defensatives laid aside, all orders for levying of forces raised; and (to the astonishment of all honest hearts), upon a petition to the houses, they prevailed, to have the Committee for safety dissolved. Thus were both the city and the Parliament drawn to act, as if they had been possessed with the most prodigious fear that ever was heard of, a fear of being safe. But it was the hand of GOD, and

this

this dementation was the fore runner of his judgment. Now did the great Officers of the army look upon themselves, as half in possession of their omnipotency, seeing this great mountain, the city, laid plain before them. But what did all this avail, so long as there were so many in the House of Commons, that would not bow the knee, nor do reverence? To scatter all appearance of opposition, the very next day, after they had sent up the aforesaid declaration, they gave fire upon the eleven members (among which myself had the honour to be one), in a general charge; and as if a *factum est* had been but due to their *dixit*, the day following, they required, that those accused members might be suspended from sitting: and a month's pay at least sent down to the army, with so much more in addition, as those Officers had received, who, in obedience to the Parliament, had yielded to disband: and that such souldiers, as had deserted the army (that is, adhered to their duty), might receive no more pay, untill the army were firſt ſerved, and their arrears diſcharged. Obedience was now become criminal, and and rebellion meritorious. For a concluſion, they did in effect enjoyn the Houſes, to raiſe no more forces, either for the relief of Ireland, or for any cauſe whatſoever, untill themſelves had firſt diſpatch'd their buſineſs, which, in their lofty ſtyle, they called the tranſaction of the kingdoms. A ſatifactory anſwer was required to all theſe particulars, as peremptorily as if they had had the Parliament in Popilius his circle.

<small>T. Livius.</small>

The ſhamefull truth is, the Houſes had now brought themſelvs into ſuch an yielding condition, that, like thoſe people that Plutarch ſpeaks of, they knew not how to ſay, No. And therefore, without conteſting, they gently vote a month's pay, as was deſired; and ſent an intimation to the Generall, and the Commiſſioners of Parliament, that they expected the army ſhould

<small>Plut. de Vitioſo Pudore.</small>

fhould, upon this, draw back unto the diftance of forty miles from London (according to the former order) and for that which concerned their members, they declared, that they were ready to receive any particulars, and to hear any witneffes that could be produced againft them. Whilft this was in difpatch, the Common Council prefented them with the draught of a letter addreffed to the Generall and the army, and requefted their approbation of it. It was drawn according to the old court rule, with a return of thanks for injuries, and fignifyed little; only it fhewed poorly, and gave a good encouragement to the army; and there was all that was in it, and all that came of it. But however (as dying people are ready to fwallow any thing) it pafs'd the Houfe, accompany'd (through the prevalency of the Independent party) with an order, that the city might have free liberty to write what letters, and fend what Commiffioners they pleafed

Sen. de Irâ, l. ii. c. 53.

pleased to the army. This was a great diminution of the honour of the Parliament, that the citizens should have a power given them, to agitate, and treat singly, as a distinct body by themselvs; and was so much taken off from that authority which quickly coms to nothing, if it be not preserv'd entire. *Nulla est, nisi tota.* I shall not presume to say more of it; GOD knows, with what affections, I have said this.

June the 22d. Upon receipt of the month's pay, the Generall wrote to the Houses, that he would very shortly call a Council of Warr, about the removal of the army unto the distance required, and then they should have a positive answer, what would be done. A fair respect! But all was to be taken without weighing, that had the stamp of the Generall and army upon it. The next day after this came up that thundering remonstrance, which in plain terms, and without types or figures, declared, that if by the morrow following

following, the eleven members were not suspended from sitting, they should be inforced to take such courses extraordinary, as God should enable them, and direct them unto: and to imbitter this, they added reprochfull expressions, concerning the dishonour and prejudice of retracting votes and ordinances; wherein they were not only guilty of the sinn of Aaron, in making the Houses naked; but of the sin of Ham, in mocking at them, when they themselvs had uncover'd them, and exposed them to their shame among their enemies. The measure thus pressed down by the army, was made to run over by the City Commissioners, who had so tuned the Common Council to a perfect unison with the army, that (as in a musical sympathy) the one moved according to the pulse and touch of the other; as appeared in that consent and accord of both their desires to the Houses, that all forces, lifted by the Committee of Safety, and the Militia, might

might be difbanded, and difcharged; and that the reduced Officers, and fouldiers, might be putt out of the lines of communication. The firft of thefe, as being nothing but a chimera, and fanfy, was eafily granted; and they, that made their boaft of that, did but (according to the old faying) hold faft, when they had taken nothing. The latter was rejected, as inconfiftent with the honour and juftice of the Parliament, to reward evil for good, to thofe that left all to adhere unto their duty; and as difadvantagious to the Houfes to deprive themfelvs of fo confiderable a ftrength, and by fuch a precipitate act, like Valentinian (as Proximus faid of him, when he had made Ætius away), to cut of one hand with another, at fuch a time, when they were like to need more hands, then ever they had done yet; and laftly, as dangerous to give fo juft an occafion of difcontent, *fortibus & miferis*, to difoblige men of courage in want, which might either

either thruft them upon fom defperate act in the city, or neceffitate them to incorporate with the army, where underhand they were already offered a fair reception.

The Houfe of Commons had formerly (as we have faid) given notice, by their Commiffioners to the army, that they expected particulars and proofs againft their members; but nothing being offered, but that infolent commination, requiring their immediat fufpenfion, without any further circumftance; it was held agreeable to confcience and equity to declare, That it did not appear, that any thing had been faid, or done by them, in the Houfe, touching any matters conteined in the papers fent from the army, for which in juftice they could be fufpended, and that by the laws of the land no judgment could be given for their fufpenfion, upon thofe papers, before particulars were offered, and proofs made. This might have been fufficient to filence all further clamour, if any thing refembling

Junii 25⁰ 1647.

sembling an obedience had been left in the army; but the Azariahs, and the Johanans, and all the proud men, were so incensed at it, that they immediately marched up to Uxbridge, within 15 miles of London; and from thence sent forth their manifesto, dated the 27th of June 1647, wherein they took the boldness to censure that vote as unjust, and contrary to precedent, and earnestly importuned that the particular charge, and proofs expected from them (which they looked upon but as tithing mint and cumin), might be laid aside (though they had them ready) untill the great things of the law, the more general matters of the kingdome, were first considered and settled; and that in the mean time those members might, by the wisedome and justice of the House, be excluded and suspended. And whereas the Houses had formerly required the army to surrender his Majesty's person into the hands of their Commissioners, that he might

might be brought to Richmond, whereby both kingdoms might have free opportunity to make application unto him, their anfwer was in plain terms, that they defired that no place might be propofed, for his Majefty's refidence neerrer London, then where they would allow the quarters of the army to be.

Things being reduced to this meafuring caft, that either the Parliament muft be affronted, or the eleven members cede to the power of the army (for to expect juftice had been vain, and not fperable, where the informants made themfelvs the judges), the members thought it became them better, to deny themfelvs by a feafonable facrificing of their own rights and priviledges, then to expofe the Houfes unto any difadvantage upon their occafion; and therefore agreed, to defire leave that they might abfent themfelvs for fix months, which, after fome debate, was granted; and the Speaker had order to give paffes for that time, unto fuch of them as had inclination

clination to transport themselvs into forrein parts. This act was enterteined in the army with such a supercilious garbe, as Cicero describes *in Piso altero ad frontem sublato, altero ad mentum depresso supercilio,* with one ey-brow screw'd up to their forehead, and the other fetch'd down to their chinn. To shew their lyonlike generosity, how much they were satisfyed with this couching (so they were pleased to interpret it), they abased themselves so low as to exalt the modesty of those gentlemen in withdrawing themselvs; though not without a nodding admonition that they hoped they would take heed how they came into the House again; and in demonstration of their good nature, they thereupon drew of their quarters further from London towards Salisbury.

Having thus gained the strong holds, and cast down the high imaginations that were against them, they thought there was but one way remaining to captivate every thought to their obedience, which was to

take

Ovid. de Trist. l. iii. Eleg. 5.

take up the publick authority (as Jehu did Jonadab) into the chariot unto them, that so carrying that countenance along with them, they might with the more ease and safety obteine their own ends. For this purpose, they wrought with the Parliament to give them a new livery, and cognisance to retein them as their army, to vote their continuance in a body, and to order provision to be made for them. All was obteined, as was desired, for there was now (according to the old proverb) but one servant in the family, and that was the master. The army servant had been so delicately brought up, that he was becom a son, or rather a master, *Dominus Domini*, as it was said of Narcissus his master's master. In the midst of this wanton fortune, when these gallants conceived themselvs past all rocks, and in a smooth water, unexpectedly the impeached gentlemen (forgetting their good manners) grew troublesome again, upon the provocation given by that bravado,

Prov. xxix. 21.

Sen. in Mort. Claudii.

vado, that the proofs were ready againſt them; but it was not yet ſeaſonable to produce them, which they look'd upon as a ſcorn, and with a ſcorne; and thereupon petitioned the Houſe, that Sir Thomas Fairfax, and the army, might be appointed, by a ſhort and peremptory day, to bring in their particulars and proofs, and that there might be a ſpeedy proceeding; which was accordingly ordered, and the Friday following aſſigned for it, being the 4th of July. This ſate ſo cloſe, that it wrung; and the army, being not able to produce any thing by that day, was fain to winch it off unto the ſixth day.

In this intervall, Commiſſary Generall Ireton, and his fellow accuſers of their brethren, were ſadly put to their invention what to charge upon them. But ſomthing of neceſſity was to be alledged, and therefore being mett together, they proceeded in this manner; Firſt, they propoſed the name of the party; and then they fell to pumping

pumping, what they fhould fay againft him.
Herein the dexterity of the Commiffary
Generall was very remarkable, who was
moft active in the framing of the charge,
and gave particular directions to the Secre-
tary, what he fhould write down againft
fuch and fuch perfons; and when fome of
the by-ftanders (being fcandalized at the
frivoloufnefs and emptinefs of thofe criminations) demanded, with fome aftonifhment,
what they meant, to fuggeft fuch things
as they themfelves knew to have no ground
of truth in them? Anfwer was made, that
it was no matter for that, and that it was
in this bufinefs, as in a Chancery Bill,
wherein, though there were never fo many
falfities, yet any one truth would be enough
to make it hold. However, they muft be
fure to caft dirt enough, and fomthing would
ftick, which would fuffice to ferve their
turn. Thefe were the wiles, and the
methods (as I may call them, in the Apof- Eph. vi. 11.
tle's language) practis'd by them, in the
forging

forging of this impeachment, as I have received the relation from two credible witnesses, persons of reputation, who were present at the whole transaction.

In this way, as I have said, having so many good workmen among them, they made a shift by that time to stitch up som particulars together, which they called a charge, and sent to the House of Commons by Colonell Scroope. It took up a long debate (more then one day) before the House could resolve what to make of it; there being no names subscribed unto it, nor proofs accompanying it, nor any thing appearing, but a meer accusation enforced by power. The truth is like some kinde of pictures, it had several aspects; one way it might look like a charge upon the eleven members; another way, it resembled an arraignment of the House of Commons, supposing them so weak and corrupt, as to be acted by particular interests. Nevertheless, in the end it was voted a charge,

and

and thereupon time given, and council affigned to the members to make their anfwer. Who were not wanting to vindicate themfelvs, both *in foro famæ*, by a particular anfwer to the articles in charge; and *in foro juris*, by a demurrer in law, put in by them the 19th of July 1647. The replication to both, from the army, was nothing: *Ex nihilo nihil.* In the ridiculous iffue of this charge, the Houfe might feem to have been deceived by the army, as Zeuxis was deceived by Parrhafius, with a fhew of a veil, caft over a piece of work, to raife a great expectation, when all the work was but a painted veil, a meer pretence, and nothing underneath it. But in plain terms, the great officers were at a fault, and knew not which way to beat it out. For they underftood from London, that they had the worft end of the ftaff, and were likely to be caft in a way of law; they look'd upon themfelvs, as *in loco lubrico*, fomthing in the condition of Haman,

Plin. Nat. Hift. lib. xxxv. c. 10.

unlikely,

unlikely, if they should begin to fall, to meet with a bait between the top and the bottom; and the Parliament and city had so closed with them, that they had not left them room enough to draw their swords; upon those compliances they had removed their quarters so far off, that they knew not upon what pretence to return.

In this distraction they resolved to seek mischief (as Benhadad did) by proposing such unreasonable and unconscionable demands, as might administer opportunity of a breach: and like Vitellius his souldiers, *Postulare, non ut assequerentur, sed causam seditioni.* The city had already (by their Commissioners) in effect made a surrender of themselvs, and all that they had, unto them. But this was not sufficient; the Committee of militia (as it was then constituted), appeared a rubb in their way. To smooth all, and that they might have nothing to hinder their cast, they demanded a revocation of that ordinance of the 4th

of

margin: 1 Kings, xx. 7.

margin: Tacit. Hist.

of May 1647, and a re-eſtabliſhment of the former Committee. Whether this were granted or denyed, it made no great difference; they had their ends upon both, like ſea-mills equally ready to grinde with the floud or ebb. If their demand were granted, they might reckon themſelvs maſters of the city (the power thereof being put into hands devoted to their ſervice): and the Parliament itſelf would be *in miſerecordiâ*, and under their lee. And probably this might breed ill blood betwixt the Parliament and city, and make ſom breach between them, which they might manage to their own advantage. If it were denyed, *ne ſic quidem male* (as the boy ſaid, when he flung a ſtone at a dog, and hitt his mother in law), they miſſed not their mark; in gaining thereby ſuch a pretence of quarrel, as might ſerve to juſtify their march up to London, where they knew the treaſure was, and where of a long time their hearts and affections were likewiſe ſet.

Plut. de Tranquil. Animi.

Whilst things were in this suspense, the eleven members, finding themselvs under that Spartan curse of procrastination, wherein they were likely to be grinded and chewed at leisure, *lentis maxilis*, without hope of being admitted to triall in any reasonable time, thought fitt to move the house again, that forasmuch as Sir Thomas Fairfax and the army had already declared, that the proceeding upon particular proofs, to make good the charge against them, would probably take up much time, and the affairs of the kingdom, in reference to those great matters proposed by them, would (as they pretended) require a present consideration; and had therefore propounded, that these general and essential matters might be first debated and setled; and in regard it was supposed, that the absence of the said members would facilitate the passage of business; they were so farr from the thought of giving interruption to those specious proceedings (well might they

end

Suetonius.

end), that they prefumed to renew their humble defires, that they might have leave, for fix months, to apply themfelvs to their private occafions; and that they might be free (fo many of them as fhould defire it) to go beyond the feas, and to have paffes granted them during that time. All being affented to, the next bufinefs that came to hand was the revocation of the ordinance for the militia of the 4th of May 1647, which could not be fo clofely carried, but that it took wind, and gave huge difcontentment to the city; where it was thought very much, that that Committee which had been ordeined by the unanimous confent of both Houfes, in a full and free feffion, to continue for a whole year, fhould fuddenly be overlaid, before it was a quarter old, without any caufe alledged; and thereupon followed that engagement, for the maintenance of the covenant, and the bringing his Majefty to London, in order to a perfonal treaty, fubfcribed by almoft an hundred

dred thoufand hands; which the Houfes voted a treafon, and declared all thofe traytors, that fhould prefume to act any further upon it. July the 22d, to put all out of queftion, that ordinance for the militia was reverfed, and a new old one drawn up, voted, tranfmitted to the Lords, and by them paffed; all this in a few hours.

But the more hafte there was in the Parliament, the lefs fpeed there was in the city; for thofe good people confidered their fafety and their priviledges, as both neerly concerned, in the continuation of thofe perfons, whom they had legally chofen and intrufted; and look'd upon themfelvs as at mercy in their eftates, if the validity of ordinances (the only fecurity they had for thofe vaft fumms they had lent unto the Parliament) fhould depend upon the mutable pleafure of an army. The truth is, this ftirring rais'd fom lees; for, upon the Monday following, July the 26th, after that the Sheriffs and

and Common Council had (in a refpectful way) prefented the humble defires of the city unto the Houfe of Commons, feconded with the like application from the apprentices (though with fome unfitting importunities), for the re-eftablifhment of the ordinance of the 4th of May, and the vacating that of the 27th inftant; and that the Houfes had not only complyed with them in both particulars, but yielded likewife to retract and annull their declaration againft the engagement above mentioned. After all, or moft of the apprentices were gone away, with good fatisfaction, fome diforderly perfons remained (as the dregs ever ftay laft) that brake into the Houfe, forced the Speaker to refume the chair, after he had adjourned; and would not fuffer any to depart, untill they had voted, that the King fhould come to London, to treat with the Parliament about a peace. What thofe people were, or by whom inftigated and fett on, I know not

(God knoweth, I know not), but by their good behaviour, I guefs them to have been of that fort, that he in Galateo dreamt, he faw breaking into an apothecary's fhop, rifling, and tafting, and fipping every thing (this purge, and t'other vomit); only there was a phial of difcretion there, which they never toucht.

The Common Council being advertifed of this infufferable infolency and violence, immediately difpatcht away the fheriffs, with the beft ftrength they could get together, in that unfetled condition of their militia, to refcue the honour of the Houfe; who, within a little while, fairly cleared the paffages, and fafely conveyed the Speaker home. The Lords adjourned their Houfe till the Friday following; the Commons theirs, till the next day morning. Againft which time, there was a ftrong guard provided by the new fetled militia; and the Houfe mett in fafety, and fate without interruption; and (Wednefday being the monthly

monthly fast) adjourned unto Friday. That day both Houses mett, according to former order; but rather like mutes then consonants, for want of their Speakers, who the day before had privatly withdrawn themselvs to the army. In this speechless condition, they were enforced to help themselves, by calling the Lord Willoughby of Parham to the wool-sack, and Mr. Pelham to the chair. Then, as nature, in suddain exigencies, calls in all the spirits to the heart, they summoned in all their members that could be found, to attend their service. For mine own part, I was then a free man, by the dispensation of the House (as I have already express'd), and looked upon a re-entry (without an invincibly necessity compelling me thereto) as an act of no less madness, then that of Ulysses, who, when he was safely gotten out of the Cyclop's den, would needs adventure in again, to fetch his hatt and girdle, which he had left behind

hind him. GOD knows my thoughts were fixed upon a quiet retreat; and in order unto that, I had written to the Generall, to have an honourable aſſurance from him, that I might in ſafety, and without moleſtation, take liberty to follow my occaſions in the country; and accordingly I received a paſs from him, under his hand and ſeal, to that effect. But before I could take poſſeſſion of that happineſs, I had a particular command brought to me by one of the ſergeant's men, that I ſhould give my attendance upon the Houſe. What I ought to have done in this dilemma, might have tried a better judgment then mine to determine. For mine own part, I conceived it to be my duty to obey the order of the Houſe, not knowing (if I had done the contrary), but that it might have been interpreted a contumacy in mee; there being no vote at all againſt my coming in, nor any thing to juſtify my abſence, but mine own voluntary withdrawing, which

was

was only to preferve the honour of the Houfe, at that time (as I have already fignified) in danger of a violation.

The Parliament was now in a gafping condition, and of thofe two fympathies in nature, the one towards confervation, the other towards perfection, was only capable of the firft, and had no other appetite but to keep itfelf in a being. To this end, the committee for fafety was raifed from the dead, to joyn with the militia of the city, with full power and authority to lift, and raife forces, to nominate officers and commanders in chief, and to iffue out arms, and ammunition, for the defence of the King, Kingdom, Parliament, and city. And to fhew how unwilling the Houfes were to engage in a new warr (if it had been poffible to avoid it), nothing was acted upon all this, untill notice came, that the army was re-advancing with their train of artillery drawn out of Oxford; that a party of both Houfes was folemnly confederated

with

with them, and resolved to run the same fortune with them, and to live and dy with them; and that the train bands of Hartfordshire, and other counties, were summoned to come in unto them: then, and not till then, the Committee began to putt things into posture, whereupon those bustlings and liftings followed.

I had rather any other pen, then mine, should relate how, in the midst of all our preparations, the Aldermen and Common Council were drawn to desert the Houses, to betray their friends, to retract their declaration, to give up their fortes, and the line next to Westminster, with the Tower and magazine, contrary to their engagement; and all this, when they had ready at their service and command, no less then eighteen regiments of foot, some of them eighteen hundred, and two thousand strong; the weakest eight hundred, which was but one, and that incomplete; all compounded of as gallant men, and as well provided for

the

the field, as any in the Chriftian world; and when they might have had (if they would themfelves) between fower and five thoufand horfe, all mounted by reformado officers, and gentlemen of quality (a force not to be numbered, but eftimated), at which time Sir Thomas Fairfax had not neer half their proportion in foot, and not above half of that half ferviceably armed; and his horfe, though ftrong enough in numbers, yet almoft in as ill equipage as his foot.

If I were mafter of that tacite oratory, in which Apollonius is faid to have been fo perfect, as that, without the trouble of fpeaking one word, he could make himfelf intelligible, I fhould here willingly choofe; *non difcendo dicere,* to exprefs the fad fenfe, which in my heart I retain of the confufions following in thofe times, and continued to this prefent, by paffing them over with a fignificant filence. But having undertaken to report the feveral acts of

Philoftrat in VitaApollon. L c. 11.

Cicero pro Cluent.

this

this tragedy, I cannot now lay my hand upon my mouth, and make an end before I have done. I touched, a little before, upon the fecession of divers eminent members of both Houfes, from the body of the Parliament, and their confederation with the army. But I hold it decent and neceffary to fay fomthing more of it (before I go off from this narrative), both in regard it was the principal encouragement, and pulley, as it were, to draw on, and accelerate the advance of the army up to London; and to the end likewife, that it may be known to the world, that the Parliament fell, neither bound nor fettered, but betraid by the infidious practices of its own members, as the Lyon in Theocritus was excoriated by his own paw. I fhall perform this with all tendernefs, and in that character of ftyle, which Heraclitus fpeaks of, *Neque dicendo, neque occultando, fed fignificando,* rather intimating, then relating particulars.

[margin: Theocrit. Idyll. 26.]

After

After that unsufferable affront putt upon the House of Commons, 26° Julii 1647 (which I have formerly mentioned), there was such offence taken, that the Earls of Northumberland, Salisbury, Denbigh; the Lords Say, Wharton, and some others; Mr. Lenthall, Speaker of the House of Commons, Mr. Pierrepoint, Sir Arthur Hesilrigg, Sir John Evelin of Wiltshire, Mr. St. John, and many more of that party withdrew privatly out of the city, by several ways, the Thursday following. The Lords held their first meeting at the Earle of Salisbury's house at Hatfield, whether they sent for the Earl of Manchester to come unto them (who was retired into Essex). From thence they went to Sion, a house of the Earl of Northumberland's neer Brainford, in order to their conjunction with the army; which was advanced up to Colebrooke, and ordered rendezvous upon Hounflow Heath. At Sion they shook hands with the above-mentioned gentle-

men

men of the House of Commons; where it was resolved, that both the Lords and Commons there mett should engage themselvs, by some publick declaration or remonstrance, to live and dy with the army. The General, and his Council of Warr, on the behalf of themselvs, and the whole army, had taken the like engagement, to stand and fall with them. The gentlemen had theirs ready drawn; Mr. Nathaniel Fines (as it is reported) made a draught of one for the Lords. But who ever did minute it, when it came to be perused by them, it was found to be defective in an essential and fundamental point; for that there was no proviso at all in it, for the maintenance of the dignity, and priviledges of their House, and for the security of the peerage, which was look'd upon as so material (considering the wilde principles of those people with whom they closed), that forthwith a clause, to supply that want, was framed and inserted in it; and the Lieutenant,

tenant Generall Cromwell, Commiffary General Ireton, and Sir Arthur Hefilrigg, were call'd upon for their concurrence with it. The Lieutenant General made anfwer with fome hefitation, that it was a matter of great concernment, and he defired further time to deliberate. The Commiffary Generall open'd himfelf with more franknefs, and faid, he was fo well fatisfied in the equity of that demand, that without any fcruple, he fhould give his prefent affent unto it, profeffing, that it was agreeable to reafon and confcience, that they fhould engage to defend thefe Lords in their rights and priviledges, who had, with fo much noblenefs, caft themfelvs upon their fortune, and therefore he was refolved for his part, to live and dy with them, in the maintenance of their intereft. Sir Arthur Hifilrigg faid little or nothing, but fhewed a diffatisfaction.

But the next day was not fo cloudy; for then the Lieutenant Generall gave in a clear

clear anfwer, the fubftance whereof was, that having confulted with his own heart and confcience (fo he called it), he was induced to concurr with what the Commiffary Generall had formerly delivered, that it was but juftice and honour that the Generall, his Council, and the army, fhould oblige themfelvs, unto the laft drop of their blood, to ftand in the defence of thofe Lords, and in maintenance of their dignity and rights, who had fo freely adventured their perfons to joyn with them: and accordingly he did there profefs (and therein he faid, he fpake his confcience), that he would engage his fervice, and life to uphold them. Sir Arthur Hefilrigg faid the like. With this fatisfaction the Lords were perfuaded to make their addreffes to the Generall, who quartered at Brainford, and there they tendred their declaration to him. Immediately after this followed the march of the army up to London, and, through it, the furrender of the Tower;

the re-eſtabliſhment of theſe Lords and Commoners, in their reſpective Houſes, &c. What became of their Lordſhipps forementioned engagement, I know not, for it was never publiſhed: but there may be ſome notice taken, that about this time there was a joint engagement printed in the name of thoſe particular Lords and Gentlemen, wherein that whole clauſe or proviſo, concerning their priviledges, is omitted, which ſhew'd the more unhandſomely, and like a deſigned falſhood, in regard both of the ſuppreſſion of that paper, and of the following actings, to the utter abolition of the peerage, notwithſtanding their obligation to maintein it.

And yet for a while after, thoſe great officers kept their countenance ſo well, that when as there was a report raiſed, that a great part of the army diſſented from that ſtipulation of theirs, to ſecure the priviledges of the Lords Houſe, they ſeemed to reſent it ſo farr, that Sir Hardreſs Waller

Waller was employed by them, in a formal way, to vindicate them from that aspersion. He came, accompanied with divers of the officers, to the barr of that House, and there, in the name of the whole army, protested against the report, as defamatory and false; and avowed their resolutions to live and dy with their Lordships, in the preservation of their dignity and rights; and in testimony of the reality of their intentions, and to shew, that being there as their representative mouth, he spake out of the abundance of their hearts; he made it their humble request, that this expression, and tender of their service, might be entred in their Lordships journal book, to remain there as a monument of their fidelity to after ages; and accordingly it was entered, and is there extant upon that record unto this day. But of this, a little may be too much. I shall say no more, but that their Lordships had ill luck to be taken with such chaff as this; to be

deceived

deceived by those who were known deceivers; and by some, who had so often forsworne themselves, that perjury was but *genus sermonis,* as natural to them as their mother tongue, and with whome there could be no dealing, upon any other security, then that which Gonsalvo thought fitt to have required from Ferdinand, King of Spain and Naples, that he should swear by that God, in whom he could make it appear that he did believe. But good natures are most easily inveigled. *Semper bonus homo tiro est.* But God had determined a judgment upon the land, and then it was not to be wondred at, if those, that should have been the stay of the tribes thereof were deceived.

Salvian. de Gub. Dei, l. iv.

Arnold. Ferron in Vit. Ludov. xii.

Martial. lib. xii. Epigr. 53.

I have now don with the tedious relation of the passages, between the Parliament and army; wherein my single aim hath been but to evince this truth, that in the whole business the Parliament was merely passive, and acted nothing but in order

order to a self defence, and a settlement of the peace of the nation: And to shew, that, whatever I did, or engaged to do, in the time of those transactions, was purely in obedience to the Parliament, and this, I thought, would appear more evidently in a continued narrative, whereby a judgment might be made, *super totam materiam*, then by picking out here and there particulars: As we judge of the imagery in a cloth of Arras, by opening the whole piece, and not by turning up a lippet, or an end of it. I deny not but that possibly I may have erred, and that very much, in the pursuance and execution of those commands, which upon several occasions I received from the Houses (in many things we offend all); but I shall humbly presume, to excuse myself *a tanto:* that those failings, whatever they were, proceeded from weakness and ignorance, not from malicious wickedness; and I shall never be ashamed to pray with Habakkuk, *pro ignorantiis,*

Jam. iii. 2.

Hab. iii. 1.

As

As for my intendments and ends, I shall not excuse, but own them; and particularly those very liftings of the reformados, and others: which though they carried a shew of hostility, and under that notion were objected against mee, as a levying a new warr; yet they were designed only for defence, according to the tenor of the above-mentioned ordinance of the 11th of June and the 3d of August 1647; and, in truth, had no other tendency, but to prevent a warr, by counterballancing the army with that force, whereby it might have been reduced to an even scale, and to terms of reason, in order to the settlement of the peace and tranquillity of the nation. If this, that I have said, may give satisfaction to honest men, I have enough; their judgment shall stand *pro populo*, in my account. As for the rest, *Quorum tot millia virum non faciunt*, as that Byzantine sophister said, I value their good or bad opinion, their praise or discommendation, at one and the same rate;

rate; whether they express themselvs for me or against me, it is all one to me. With me, it is a very small thing that I should be judged of them, or of man's judgment *(judicium humanum vix alphabetum illius Divini).* Yea, I judge not mine ownself: for I know nothing by myself, yet I am not hereby justified; but he that judgeth me is the LORD.

<small>1 Cor. iv. 3, 4.</small>

But *fugam fecit!* it is again objected, that upon the miscarriage of those evil designes, I fled the kingdom, making over and transporting great summs of money, which I had gotten in the warr. Concerning my departure out of the land, shortly this. The impeached gentlemen were so farr from running away upon the approche of the army, that after the city was surrendered, they stayed divers days in expectation of the worst that could be charged upon them. But hearing of nothing in question against them, and seeing nothing in agitation, but the setling the new

new conqueft, they did not think themfelvs obliged to make a ftand (like thofe vain Celtique Gauls) againft fuch a tide as was broken in; where nothing was to be expected but a perifhing to no purpofe. And thereupon Mr. Hollis, Sir William Lewis, Sir Philip Stapleton, Sir John Clotworthy, Mr. Walter Long, and myfelf, went in a free and open way to the Speaker, and took out our paffes under his hand, according to the order of the Houfe, and with the fame freedom and opennefs moft of us went out of the town at noon-day, and in a company with fifteen or fixteen horfe, which was neither a time nor an equipage likely to favour an efcape. The occafion of our taking fhipping at a private creek in Effex, was upon an intimation given us, that we were way-laid at Gravefend by the forces of the army; and therefore we refolved rather to put ourfelvs upon the mercy of the raging fea, than upon the madnefs of the people. Neither was this caution

_{Nic. Damafcen. de mor. Gent.}

caution needleſs; for notwithſtanding our paſſes, we were purſued by land, chaſed, and taken at ſea, brought back (almoſt out of Calice road) into the Downs, examined and ſearched, and (when nothing criminal could be found in us) diſcharged, by the vote of a council of warr, held abord the Vice Admiral Battin; and left to take our unhappy fortunes, with the loſs of that gallant gentleman, Sir Philip Stapleton, who was meerly kill'd by the inconveniences of that journey.

As for that ſuggeſtion, that I ſhould make over, or tranſport with me great ſumms of money; it is as untrue, as that fiction of the butter barrels was ridiculous. I acknowledge the ſending of ſome goods of mine into the Low Countries, to Rotterdam, about two or three months (if I remember not), before I was inforced, to take that courſe with myſelf; all was nothing but houſhold ſtuff, the beſt part whereof I had (by the care of a good friend) ſaved

saved out of Winchester castle, but a few hours before the King's party seised upon it, and the rest I had bought at London; but there was neither penny of money, nor ounce of plate, that travailed with it. But whatever there was, it was viewed, and allowed at the Custome-house, before the ship went off with it, which I hope may serve to give satisfaction to all reasonable people, that I meant plainly and honestly, and may shew, that there was nothing acted to put any cheat upon the state. I might add, that this was no such singular act of Providence in me; but that divers others (both Lords and Gentlemen) did the like, and no exceptions at all taken. But when men have once enterteined a prejudicate opinion, they are apt to lay condemnation upon names, and to decry whatever such or such a man saith, or doth, though they pass by the same thing in others; or it may be, say or doe it themselvs. So Erasmus observed, that the same tenets were con- demned

<small>Erasm. in Epist. ad Card. Mogunt.</small>

demned in Luther for heretical, which in St. Bernard and Auſtin were allowed for orthodox and pious.

I ſhould not forget myſelf ſo farr, as to remember the tale of the butter-barrels, but that I finde it hath left ſome impreſſion in men's minds; and what fools have fancied, wiſe men are apt to believe. I know not how to anſwer the ridiculouſneſs of it in a ſerious way, without being *ſapiens in re ſtulta*; which is the fulſomeſt kind of folly in the world. To laugh at it, inſtead of anſwering it, were but *contumeliæ contumeliam facere*, and the ſcores were quitt. But I would not be ſcandaliz'd in jeſt; *aliquid hæret*. The boys in Plutarch ſtruck the froggs in jeſt, but the poor froggs ſuffered in earneſt. To anſwer therefore the fool according to his folly, I ſhall ſay this, and maintein it, that there was neither truth, nor ſhadow of truth in that report. All that gave occaſion to this ſtrange phenomenon, was the

ſtopping

Marginalia:
Senec. Conſol. ad Helv. c. xiii.

Prov. xxvi. 5.

stopping of a summe of money at Gravesend, that (upon examination) was said to be designed for the redemption of captives at Algier; and, it seems, was barrel'd up, as if it had been a commodity of butter; and no body at that time appearing to own it, some, out of the liberality of their malice, were pleased to entitle me to it, upon no other ground of reason (that I could ever learn) but that I had formerly disposed of some goods into Holland, and therefore, in likelyhood, I might send some money after, and therefore that might be my money; a reason without sense! but it served well enough to create a belief, that I had made an advantage of the miseries of those times, to feather mine own nest: and that was enough to draw envy and malice upon me, which was the end they aimed at.

I must here take leave to speak in the language of St. Paul, to such as can have the noble patience, as to read these lines,

Would

2 Corinth. xi. 1. Would to God, ye could suffer a little my foolishness. I would be glad to give in a particular of my estate, and to deliver up my accounts, that in the trial it might evidently appear, in what condition I have subsisted during these troubles; and how farr I have been, from enriching myself at the publick cost. Possibly it may seem an impertinency; but what I do, that will I do, that I may cutt off occasion from them that desire occasion. I praise GOD for that portion which he hath given me under the sun, which (though farr from so great as the opinion of the world would make it) is not so little, but that in peaceable times it hath always afforded me a competency with comfort: in the warr, and in this miscalled peace, that hath followed it, suffered with the publique: the same wind that raiseth a storm at sea, maketh a rough and troubled water in little ponds and puddles. I may justly avow (and I can make it good) that what through the common

mon calamities that have befallen the state, and what through the malice and power of mine enemies, I have been endammaged to the value of above thirty thousand pounds, and so streightned in my subsistence, that many times I have been enforced to sell, and borrow, to buy bread. But it may be replied, that what I lost in the hundred, I got in the shire; the employment which I held in the service of the Parliament, served to make up all breaches in my private fortune. I hope I shall never outlive good nature so farr, as not to acknowledge with humble thankfulness, the large and honourable enterteinment which I received from the state. But I desire withall it may be considered, that as the goods in- *Eccles. v. 11.* creased, so they increased that eat them; and that little more accrued to me, saving the beholding them with mine eys. I was necessitated to live above mine own condition, that I might not live below that quality which the favour of the Parlia-

ment

ment had putt upon mee; so that what I receiv'd, I spent; and much I spent before I receiv'd it. A considerable part of mine arrears, amounting to above one thousand pounds, I freely remitted (upon the passing of my accompt); when the House of Commons would have allowed it; and a remaining part of it (to the summe of eight hundred pounds), I was glad to compound for, at twelve shillings in the pound, when I was a prisoner at St. James's.

All that I got in the warr, by way of purchase, or booty, was one month's pay (as a Colonel of Horse), upon the surrender of Chichester, when by the capitulation, all the officers and souldiers that were with mee, received equally the like proportion, according to their respective qualities. I had likewise seven hundred pounds for my part, of the salvage of a shipp, that was driven on ground neer Arundell, when I lay before the castle; of which I gave the House a clear information, when I deliver'd liver'd in my accompt. Befides this, of gift (at feveral times), I received one hundred pounds, from Mr. Dunch of Pufy, as I take it, who, with a great deal of kindnefs, fent it to mee (though a ftranger and utterly unknown to him), when I lay at Newbridge; and fifty pounds I had prefented to me from the town of Lewes, in acknowledgment of my poor fervice at Arundell (which I likewife reported to the Houfe); and in plate, at Gloucefter, Hereford, and Poole, to the value of about one hundred pounds, or one hundred and fifty at the moft. And this is the utmoft reckoning I can make (if it were my laft reckoning), except I fhould put to account every horfe gotten from the King's party, upon the fervice, and bring in a little painted cabinet, and fome toyes, worth twelve or fourteen pounds, prefented to my wife by the merchants of that forementioned fhip, as a token of their thankfulnefs, for the care I had fhewed to preferve their goods.

But to conclude this part, I think it may be some demonstration, that I was little the richer for all these gettings, and not likely to be guilty of sending over treasure in barrels, or of carrying it with mee in cloak baggs (as was idly and foolishly given out by them that pursued mee, after I had taken shipping), when I was fain to borrow of a good friend of mine, to make up the summe of six and fourty pounds, to carry mee into Holland. That was all the money (I take GOD to witness), that I transported out of the kingdome with mee. Some further supply of about fower or five hundred pounds (and that the uttermost), my poor wife brought after mee; but both that summe, and all the rents I could receive out of my estate I spent abroad, and made hard shift to subsist with that maintenance. I should be ashamed to lay open these particulars, but that I had rather suffer under the disreputation of a beggery, then ly under a misopinion,

that

that I have, to the value of a ſhoo-latchet, enriched myſelf by any baſe advantage. And therefore my hope is, that (taking in all circumſtances) it will appear evidently, that my butter barrels were empty, or they would never have made ſo much ſound; and that my eſtate is in no ſuch envious condition, as to give any man a juſt reaſon to think, or ſuſpect I have in the leaſt meaſure improved it, at the expence of the publique.

And now one would think, after all this hue and crie, this purſuit by land and ſea, I might have had leiſure given me to make a ſtand upon the further ſhore, as Abner did upon the top of the hill, and to call, How long ere the people return from fol- *2 Sam. ii. 26.* lowing their brethren? But it was not my fortune to meet with Joab's good nature. I quickly found thoſe ſeas were too narrow to ſtop the paſſage of malice after mee. For notwithſtanding all the circumſpection I could uſe (and I uſed all I could), it was impoffible for mee to fecure myfelf from the ftrife of tongues. Somtimes I was reported to be in Scotland; fomtimes to be in France; fomtimes to be in both places at once; when all that while I lived quietly at Leyden, or harmlefly at the Hague. I thank GOD I was fo well fortifyed, that the found of thofe fhaken leavs did not difturbe me; but only ferved to put me in mind of a piece of Ariftotle's doctrine, That lies might be contradictories, never truths. But there are three particulars, which I find the charity of that time would moft willingly have ftuck upon mee, during my abode in thofe forraigne parts; firft, that I fhould then have taken a commiffion from the prince that then was; fecondly, that I fhould have had a hand in the revolt of the fhips; thirdly, that I was interefted in the Scottifh engagement. To thefe I fhall crave leave to make a fhort and a clear anfwer, which muft be with a flatt negative to all.

For

For the first, they that were acquainted with my going over, can bear mee witness, in what a dilemma I was, what way to take, whether into France, or into the Low Countries; and that nothing cast mee upon the latter, but the single consideration, that in those parts I might be more out of the way of the royal party; with which (as things then stood) I knew not how to joyn, and was unwilling to clash. My manner of life in Holland was sufficiently known, how that for the greatest part of my time which I spent there, I lived in a retired way, and almost in the condition of an inclusiary at Leyden; *Lucullus cum Lucullo*, myself with myself. It is true, after I came to the Hague, whether I was necessitated to remove, for som particular reasons, meerly concerning mee in my private family, I looked somthing more abroad then I had formerly done, I could not choose but pay my homage to that queen of women, the Queen of Bohemia, whom I had the honour to serve at Prague, in the firſt breaking out of the German warr. I could do no leſs then return civilities, when I received them from gentlemen, and I could not refuſe to receive them from ſome, that had born arms for the King, except I would have denounced a warr with the whole party, and have made them mine enemies upon no other ground, but becauſe they ſhewed an inclination to be my friends, which had been little diſcretion in mee, and leſs honeſty. If there were a fault in this, it muſt be upon their account, that expoſed mee to ſuch a condition, that I muſt live either at the mercy or courteſy of enemies. But notwithſtanding all court-ſhip, and compliments, I defy the worſt of malice to prove, that ever I took any commiſſion from the prince, or acted, or counſelled to act any thing in violation of my covenant, or tending to the diſſervice of the parliament.

As to the revolt of the ſhips, the great
GOD

God of heaven knows I never heard syllable of it, till it was common news, and matter of discourse in every barber's shop in the Hague. And (if I have any thing of a Christian in mee) I was never directly nor indirectly acquainted with the designe, before it brake forth, nor of counsell with it after, and so jealous I was of dipping my stopp in that platter, that when the fleet came to Helvoer Sluys (but a few hours distance from the Hague), I never once went to see it; and when the Captains, and gentlemen, that commanded it, made their application to the court, I never communicated with them, nor with any one person among them, in any thing of advice, or correspondence, in order to the carrying on of that engagement. And this is true, as I shall answer it to the God of truth, at the last day.

Touching the Scottish engagement, I shall speak no further then in relation to myself. I acknowledge that I have, and ever

ever have had, a particular respect and value for that nation. I love their constancy to their covenant, their steadiness in their counsells, their gallantry in the field. Some of them I have had the honour to command, and braver men, I am confident, no man could command. I could willingly enlarge myself to further expressions, but that in so doing, I might be thought to follow mine own passion; as it was said of Androcydes the painter, that he was so elaborate in picturing the fishes about Scylla, only because he loved fish so much. True it is, that in these latter years it hath pleased the high Disposer of all things, to lay the honour of that people strangely in the dust, even to the stupefaction and astonishment of the world. But yet with a *salvo* to the generosity, and bravery of the nation, be it spoken, their destruction hath been from themselvs; from their own unhappy partialities and emulations, whereby it may be said of them, in the language

of

Plut. Sympos. l. iv.

of Salvian, *Prius perierant, quam perirent.* They were undone by themselvs, before they could be undone by others; and it is a sad addition to their calamity, that they are not, *miseri sine crimine.*

_{Salvian. de Gub. Dei, l. vi.}

_{Ovid Meta. l. iii.}

But notwithstanding all this, a lion is a lion though his paws be never so much pared. As to the judgment of GOD, in these mystical dispensations, I lay my hand upon my mouth. Secret things belong unto him. They that trouble themselvs, because they cannot discypher the characters of his providence, nor read the reason of his doings, may in the sense of their own infirmities and weakness, finde the reason why they cannot finde the reason. It is enough for mee to know, that though the ways of GOD be in the clouds, dark and imperceptible unto us, yet they are uncorrupt: his judgments may be secret, but they are always just. My charity binds me to believe, that the goodwill of him that dwelt in the bush will preserve that people,

_{Psal.xviii.30.}

people, in this firy trial, and make it an occasion to refine, not to confume them. However for myfelf, I would have it known, that I am an Englifhman, and the fon of an Englifhman, and no confideration fhall ever make me forfeit that intereft. Shortly, for the engagement in queftion, I never had to do with it, directly, nor indirectly, and I fhall look upon it as an advantage to mee, to be queftioned for it.

I have now runn through all the particulars objected againft mee (fo farr as my intelligence could reach), and according to my weaknefs (but yet according to truth), I have made my anfwer. It is my humble defire, that what I have faid, may be evenly weighed, and let juftice hold the fcales, I mean the juftice of a free Parliament, unto which I appeal, and where only I ought to be judged. For if I have don wrong, or committed any thing worthy of death, or of bonds, I refufe not to dy, or to fuffer imprifonment: but if there be none of thofe those things, whereof I am accused, no other power can of right touch mee. The plain truth of all is, that these charges and criminations were but so much noise, and were made use of by the great officers of the army for no other end and purpose, then as Theo the painter made use of a trumpetter, to sound a charge, before he would put to shew his picture of a man at arms lively drawn, as ready to engage: that is, only to raise fansie and expectation; for by these airs and fames, they prepossessed peoples minds with apprehensions of they knew not what; that they might the better sett off, and glorify the engagement, and infall of their men at arms, upon the House of Commons, on the 6th of December 1648, when, amongst divers others, members of that House, they were pleas'd to seise upon mee, and to make mee their prisoner. Till then (as they themselvs professed in their humble answer) there was nothing acted in relation to the Parliament,

Ælian. Var. Hist. L. ii. c. 44.

or

or any member thereof. All former clamors against mee were but so many fanfaras and flourishes; but that vote of the 5th of December was the sin against their holy Spirit never to be forgiven.

To exasperate the army further against mee at that time, some false tongues among them had raised a report, that I had defrauded the state, and interverted great summs of money to mine own use, which should have been paid in to the army. Wherein, I may say, they used mee, as the persecutors of old used the primitive Christians, when they cased them in beast skins, and exposed them to be baited as beasts; first they clothed mee with reproach and dishonour, and as it were put the beast upon mee, and then in that disfigured case, sett the army on to worry mee.

<small>Tacit. Annal. l. xv.</small>

For answer to those calumniations, as to the point of my concurrence with that vote above mentioned, I am so farr from denying,

denying, or retracting it, that I own it, according to Job's expreſſion, as my crown, as my honour; and with comfort I can remember I gave my Yea to it, that laſt night of the laſt Parliament that ever ſate in England, with the ſame peace of conſcience wherewith I deſire to deliver up my laſt breath unto GOD. If it were a crime to vote, that his Majeſty's anſwer to the propoſitions at Newport was a ground for the Houſe to proceed upon for the ſettlement of the peace of the kingdom; there was no honeſt man but had reaſon to thank all that were guilty of it, *Crimine te potui demeruiſſe meo.* It was, to ſpeak in the language of Pliny, *Unicum crimen eorum qui crimine vacabant,* the only guilt of thoſe that were innocent. The reaſons inducing that vote, and the juſtification of it, are already publiſh'd to the world, in the vindication of the impriſoned and ſeluded members; and in that excellent and unanſwerable ſpeech, delivered that 5th of December, *Job xxxi. 36.* *Ovid.*

December, in the House of Commons, by Mr. Prinne; and therefore I shall say nothing to it, but therefore only, because I can say no more but what hath been already said. As to that base report of my having been false to the state, I can do no less then stick the lye upon it. For I never touched penny of the publick money, but what I received for mine own enterteinment from the hands of the Treasurer, or Commissary; and for which I had, long before that time, accompted to the Parliament.

I have not ranked these two last particulars, with the former charges that were against me, because I cannot esteem the first any crimination at all, but a commendation; and if I had as many lives as I have hairs upon mine head, I would sacrifice them all to the maintenance of it; and for this second, it was an arrow that flew in the darke, no body appearing to own it; and besides, it was but in effect a

second

second part to the tune of the same suggestion formerly mentioned, that I had enriched myself upon the advantage of the times, and treasur'd up great summs of money in forrein parts. Only it was the more maliciously timed, in that juncture, to enrage the souldiers against mee; as I found by their good usage of mee, when I was in their custody at St. James's. And unto this, having already made my defence, I shall use no vain repetition, but referr myself to what I have said before. Only for conclusion of this part, I cannot but observe, upon the whole matter, the traversers and cross ways that I have met with in my passage through these pikes. In March 1647, Sir John Clotworthy and I received publique thanks from the House of Commons, for our report made concerning the petition of the army, and in June following wee were both impeached for it. In the same month again I had my share of thanks among the eleven members,

bers, for withdrawing out of the Houſe, and in February following I was diſmembred for not coming into the Houſe. In Auguſt 1647, I was put into a baniſhed condition, becauſe it was alledged, that I would have levyed a new warr, and in December 1648, I was impriſoned, becauſe I voted for a new peace. In this labyrinth, what ſhall I doe or ſay: *Dirige greſſus meos, Domine.* Let me be wiſe enough to be honeſt, and I deſire no more.

Thus much for the relation of what I have acted from time to time, according to the orders, and for the ſervice of the Parliament; wherein I may ſay, with Job, I have declared the number of my ſtepps, I have given a particular and a juſt accompt of all my proceedings, as farr as poſſible I could. In the next place, I ſhall (as in a civil ſhrift, or confeſſion) lay open the ſecrets of my heart, my affections, my judgment, mine ends, that it may be known what I am in the inner man; and that it may

Job xxxi. 37.

may appear, that I have not at any time, for any diftafts, or provocations whatfoever, forfaken my firft love, nor dealt falfely in my covenant.

In the multitude of my thoughts within mee, this comfort hath refrefhed and delighted my foul; that after that way which others are pleafed to call faction and party, I have walked in the finglenefs and integrity of mine heart, according to the principles upon which I firft engaged. I fpeak it not, as juftifying myfelf, *in foro cæli*; (I know well, that in the prefence of God, my beft actions are but in the rank of my leaft finns). But as to this generation of people, that are (according to the fenfe of that text, which fome fay our Saviour wrote Matth. vii. 3. with his finger upon the ground) fo quick-fighted to efpie the mote that is in their John ix. 41. brother's eye, and fo blinde as not to fee the beame which is in their own eye, whofe fin remaineth. And truly the more innocent I finde myfelf, the bolder I fhall be be with them; *Quanto innocentior, tanto frontosior*, as it was said of Janus. Those whited walls may smite me on the mouth, but they shall never stop my mouth till they stop my breath. They shall not take away my rejoicing, that I have, in all good conscience, served God, untill this day, both in the maintenance of my covenant, and in my sufferings for it.

In testimony whereof, and to evidence my devotion to the grounds and ends of that engagement, I do hereby solemnly declare, in the presence of GOD, and his holy Angels, that I am still constant in my desire, to see the Church setled in doctrine, discipline, and government, that it may no longer fluctuate up and down (like that temple of Apollo) in an uncertain condition, agitated with the whirlewinds of new old heresies, and errors, in perpetual hazard of splitting upon schisms and separations: but may, in GOD's good time, recover

Pomp. Mela.

ver the fair havens of peace and truth. In order to that end, I do zealously wish that the whole Church were reduced to such unity and consonance of judgment, that all animosities and discriminations laid aside and discharged, we might hear no more the language that I am of Paul, and I of Apollo, and I of Cephas, but be all one in CHRIST. It might befitt the mouth of a great Turk well enough to say, that variety of opinions became his empire, as well as variety of flowers became his garden. But GOD, who is over all, higher then the highest, and one both in essence and in name, hath under that prohibition to the Israelites, not to sow mingled seed in their fields, tacitly, and by implication forbidden commixtures of religion, in his garden, the Church; and therefore I abominate a promiscuous toleration of all sects, and professions in it, as inconsistent either with purity or unity, the beauty and bands thereof; and as indeed the principal cause

1 Corinth. 1. 12.

Lev. xix. 19.

of

of atheism in this our age, wherein men of corrupt minds, taking offence at the discordant and cross opinions that are among us, do grow to a contempt of all religion, and to think of the several professors thereof (as St. Paul puts the case, an unlearned person, or an unbeliever, would judge, if he came into a congregation where they spake with several tongues) that they are all mad.

1 Cor. xiv. 23.

But here I would be understood, *cum grano salis*. There may be different characters of parties in the church; one may say, I am the LORD's, and another may call himself by the name of Jacob. Some may be intitled Episcopians, some Presbyterians, and some Independents; and yet all be Israelites indeed, belonging to the same election of grace, and (as it is written of the Novatian faction, and the orthodoxe Christians of that time) they may all jointly contribute materials to the building up of our temple; and therefore it would be necessary

Isai. xliv. 5.

Socrat Hist. l. ii. c. 30.

fary to have a fitt diftinction held, between thofe, whofe tenets are deftructive to the fundamentals, the effentials of religion, the *prima credibilia* (as they call them); and thofe who differ from us only in circumftances and deduced points. To the firft, there is no place to be given, no not for an hour; there is not fo much as the civility of a God-fpeed to be allowed them but as enemies to the Crofs of Chrift, they are to be profecuted with Anathema Maranatha. There can be no arbitrament made between GOD and the Devil. But as to thofe who are divided from us, only in things indifferent, in matters only ceremonial and ritual (though I could wifh in my heart, that even in thofe particulars there were fuch an agreement as might produce an uniform contemplation of CHRIST among us); yet I cannot but think, there fhould be much tendernefs and condefcenfion ufed towards them. Certainly that frame of fpirit is moft conformable

2 Joh. *.

formable to our Saviour's temper, who would not have his believing little ones offended. It is the Apostle's rule, that those that are strong ought to bear the infirmities of the weak, and not to please themselvs, but others for their good unto edification. And it was the Apostolical practise, in that first Council at Jerusalem, not to impose any thing upon the Church, but what was of necessary observation; and even in those very particulars which they did enjoyn, it is remarkable, that they exacted not any rigid obedience, but with allowance of a prudential latitude. Upon which ground, St. Paul (notwithstanding the canon in dispensation of circumcision) took Timothy, and circumcised him; because of the weak Jews which were in those quarters, that he might gain them by that compliance; and the whole Church, not long after, assumed the like freedome, to lay by those other acts concerning abstinence from meats offered to idols, and from blood

Matth. xviii. 6.
Rom. xv. 1, 2.

Act. xvi 3.

blood, when the caufes and confiderations upon which they were paffed (which referred to the fuperftition of the Jews, and the coalition of the Gentils with them) were removed, and taken away.

This was the Chriftian liberty of the primitive times, even in thofe things, which, at their firft inftitution, were held neceffary. As for matters of bare form, and politie and difcipline, they were never then look'd upon as of the freehold of religion, annexed to the effence of it; but as in the nature of moveables, which might be parted with, *falvo contenemento* (according to the language of the law), and therefore they were not impofed with any neceffary and penal obligation, but left to fpiritual difcretion, to be varied, as times and places, and accidents fhould require. Accordingly we read of divers ancient cuftoms in the church (fuch as were the adminiftration of the communion to infants, the trine immerfion in baptifme, the not fafting

Caffand. in defenf. Offic. pii Viri.

fasting, and not kneeling between Easter and Whitsuntide, night vigils, and others), that have been since, upon good grounds, and without offence, abolished. We read of several churches that have instituted and reteined their several rites, as the churches of Alexandria and Thebais, that used to receive the communion after super; that of Antioch in Syria, that observed praying to the west; that of Rome, that observed their Saturday fasts, contrary to the manner of all other churches, and yet none of them censured for their inconformity. St. Augustine was of opinion, that all churches were to be left free, to the use of their own customs, though it were but for this reason, that by their multiformity, people might be convinced that rites and ceremonies were not of the substance of religion, and that religion was not tied to them.

In those good days, a difference about a formality made no difference in point of charity. Witness the example of Anicetus and

Niceph. l. iv. c. 39.

and Polycarpus; the one Bishop of Rome, the other of Smyrna; who, though they differed both in opinion and practise, about the celebration of Easter, yet when Polycarpus came to Rome, upon occasion of the difference, Anicetus received him as a brother, and ceded to him so farr, as to let him officiate in his own church. This unity of the spirit, in the bond of peace, continued to Pope Victor's time, who was the first that compelled conformity in ceremonials, but he was sufficiently reproved for it by Irenæus, upon this ground, that the observation of such things ought to be free. And yet all the violence of that Pope could not prevail so much, but the doctrine of Christian liberty was defended, and mainteined both by Irenæus and others, and so continued in the church, untill after the Council of Nice. It is true, in the following ages, Charles the Great enforced the observation of the Romish rites, upon his subjects, *cum minis & supliciis*. And Alphonso

Euseb. Hist. l. v. c. 24.

Catalog. Test Verit. fol. 10.

Fox. Acts, and Mon.

Naucler. Gener. 22.

Ph. Mornay de Euchar. l. i. c. 8.

Alphonſo the Sixth, King of Spain, did the like in his dominions: but it was with the infinit regret of their people; and both of them hear ill for it to this day.

I am therefore againſt the ſevere, and (I think) unrectifyed zeal of thoſe that do not only preſs theſe things upon men's conſciences by the neceſſity of a commandment, which GOD hath left at large; but exact obedience to their injunctions, with ſanguinary penalties. This is to make our Saviour a Moloch, or an heathen idol, as if he were pleaſed with humane ſacrifices, which he abhorrs. It is obſervable, that when Anti-chriſt is to be deſtroyed and conſumed, it ſhall not be *ore gladii* but *ſpiritu oris*; it ſhall not be by force of arms, but by the powerfull operation of the word; *per linum*, according to that propheſy of the Sibyll, that is, *per chartam* (as Theodor Bibliander expoundeth it) *cujus materia eſt linum maceratum*; by paper, by the written word of GOD: and if, in points fundamental

mental and of fubftance in religion, if in the oppofition to Antichrift himfelf, there be fo much tendernefs to be ufed; then certainly, in things, Adiaphorus, in middle and indifferent things, there is much more to be indulged. We muft therefore beware, that in procuring and muniting this unity in the church, as to exterior forms of worfhip and ecclefiaftical politie, we do not offend any of thofe little ones, who cannot, out of confcience, or will not (it may be) out of weaknefs, come up to us precifely, in every degree and minute, and fcruple of rite and ceremony, leaft otherwife, while we heave too eagerly and violently at every irregular twigg, we make the axe head fly from the helve, and chance to deftroy our brother, for whom CHRIST dyed. In this cafe, our Saviour's rule is obfervable, which is, in things material and doctrinal, to account thofe againft us, that are not with us; but in things only formal, and of circumftance, to reckon

thofe

those with us, that are not against us, I wish it were better followed.

But yet again (if I may have leave to speak my wishes); I would not have this grace turned into wantonness. I could wish, that in declining those ceremonies and rites, which carry an appearance of superstition and vanity, men would not run into a contrary extreme of irreverence, neglect, and profaness. Such humorists there were anciently; and I wish there were not so many of them now, *Qui vocant prostrationem disciplinæ, simplicitatem*; that call, or rather miscall, the prostration and abolition of all exterior discipline and ceremony, by the name of Christian simplicity and primitive purity. But certainly there is a weight in those words, *omnia decenter*. God delights to be served in a sober, but yet orderly, and comly way; and as he is not taken with pompe and ostentation: so he abhorreth sordidness, and flutterie in his church, as well as in his camp.

1 Cor. xiv. 40.

camp. No Christian church in the world is, or can be, without the use of some ceremonies. Indeed the principal glory thereof is, *ab intus*; but yet there is *varietas in veste*; decent orders and forms help to adorn it. For my own part, I am not, nor ever was, against a modest dress of religion: but I like not affected decorations. Those artifices (like the wanton dress of that woman that gave offence to Pambo) shew, as if there were more care taken to please men than to please God. Eccles. Hist. l. viii. c. 1.

For the better removing all offences of this nature, and in order to the peace of the church, it were good that were some regulation of ceremonies, as that 1st, they might not be too numerous, and so burthensom. 2d, That they might not be incongruous to the rules of faith, and so scandalous. 3d, That they might not tend to superstition, but unto edifying. And 4th, That they might not be vitiated in their practife, and made real parts of the worfhip and fervice of GOD; but be left arbitrary as indifferencies, *fine obligatione ad culpam*. If thefe cautions might be obferved in the admiffion of our ritual forms, *ubi ftimulus?* But I fubmit to better judgments. As to that which is urged by fome, that all church orders fhould be reduced to the primitive inftitutions, I like it well in doctrinals which concern the body of religion, wherein there fhould not be the leaft fhadow of a change allowed: but for outward circumftances, which are but the accoutrements and modes of the church, this precifenefs would be both mifbecoming and prejudicial to the conftitution of it; as it would appear, not only ftrange and uncouth, but be difagreeable to our complexions, and hurtfull to our healths, if, becaufe our firft parents were clad with coats of fkins, fitted for them by GOD himfelf, wee fhould quitt our prefent habits, and

and go like them, only upon the account, that what they wore was the primitive fashion, and of divine inftitution.

To clofe this difcourfe.—If ever it fhould pleafe GOD to reftore the Parliament and affembly to a being again, I could heartily wifh (I prefume not to advife). The in- ferior angels, if we believe the fchools, take not upon them to illuminate thofe of a fuperior Hierarchy: but I could wifh with all humblenefs), that the affembly might be enlarged to a general fynod of all the reformed churches, with admiffion of a fitt number of divines of all parties; and that all points in controverfy might therein receive their full determination. Whereby, in my poor opinion, there would be a double advantage gained; the one to the church, in the authority of fuch a fanction, which would involve all intereft, and filence all oppofition: and the other to the ftate, in the additional and fubfi- diary ftrength that would accrue unto it,

Aquin. 1. p. q. 106. a. 3.

by

by a firm conjunction and union of the Protestant Party throughout all Christendome; whose swords would be engaged to defend what their trowells had helped to build with us. But then, if we would have this meeting signify any thing, it must be free, as well as general. For if none but those of the predominant partie govern in it, they will make it but the second part of the Council of Trent; and deal with all dissenters from their interest (as Luther jested at the summoning of that council), much like unto them that delude a dog with a crust and a knife; who insteed of bestowing the bread upon him, which they seem to promise, make him feel the weight of the haft. I confess, that according to the present aspect and configuration of affairs, there is but very little hope appearing, that those or any other wishes of this kinde should be likely to prove effectuale. But that desperation begets my hope, that it may be time for the LORD to work,

Quia

Quia necesse est, ibi adesse divinum, ubi cessat humanum consilium. Joseph Antiq. l. 18. c. 10. The good LORD, in his good time, shew mercy to the afflicted estate of this church; even for his sake, who in all our afflictions is afflicted. *Miserere Domini nostri JESU CHRISTI*; as Luther prayed.

I hold myself obliged by the laws of the land, the oath of allegiance, and the covenant (as by a threefold cord), to the preservation of monarchy, with all the just rights and prerogatives thereunto belonging. This is so plain and evident, that, like a mathematical demonstration, it is not to be proved, but granted. What laws have we, or ever had, but either regal, or imperial? Those of the Romans, Mercians, West Saxons, Danes, Northumbrians, Normans, have all the impression of the crowne upon them; and nothing is current for legal among us, but under that stampe. It is true the ordinances of Parliament have been taken as obligatory, in cases of extreme necessity, *pro tempore*. But they are not

not of force to binde as laws, *ad semper*, without the King's concurrence. And therefore it was, upon a rational ground, desired by the army, in their above mentioned representations, March 1646, that the royal assent might be procured to their ordinance of indemnity, as well knowing, that without this signature, nothing could be firmly established. Bracton hath a saying out of Justinian, *Lex facit, ut ipse sit Rex*; and it will bear an inversion, *Rex facit, ut ipsa sit Lex*. All our bills are but crude conceptions, untill they be quickned by *Le Roy le veult*. In this sense we may say, The King's Will is our Law.

As for the oath of allegiance, and the covenant, they do not cross one another (as hath been rightly declared by the Assembly of Divines and both Houses, in their exhortation to take the covenant), but, like a double lock, they serve more firmly to engage men in the preservation and defence both of the person of the King (for the time being), and of the

royal

royal authority: and however som would elude this obligation in the covenant, by wresting the words (in the preservation and defence of the true religion and liberties of the kingdom) to a restriction of the engagement, for the preservation and defence of the Kings authority, as if it should be no further binding then as it may be consistent with the maintenance of religion and liberty. Yet that is upon a presupposition, that religion and liberty are inconsistent with that authority, which is a principle that will never be granted, and can never be proved. God knows, I took the covenant, as I took the oath of allegiance, without equivocations, or mental reservations, and all the construction I can make of that clause (except I would lame it with straining it) is no more but that, together with the preservation, and defence of religion and liberty, I vow to preserve and defend the King's authority, the particle in, being there merely conjunctive, and referring equally both to the one and the other. I think, I may say of the sense of this passage, as Maldonat saith of the 2d of Luke, v. 34, *Nescio, annon facilior hic locus fuisset, si nemo eum exposuisset.* It would have been plain enough if it had not been expounded.

But besides these obligations of law and gospel (as I may say), that binde mee, there is enough in reason to persuade mee to the maintenance of monarchical government; both as it is in itself a form of of politie, the most ancient and natural; and as it is unto this nation, of all others, the most congenial. For the antiquity thereof, not to speak of the divine monarchy of GOD, in the universal world; and of CHRIST in the Catholique Church, further then to inferr, that that kinde of regiment must needs, according to a square of reason, be the most exact and perfect, which hath in it the neerest approche and conformity to the kingdome of GOD, and his CHRITS: It is a truth, as clear as the sun, and within two days as old, that the original donation

donation of government is from GOD, and was by him settled and vested upon man, in consideration of the divine image impressed upon him at his creation. The words of the grant are express; GOD said, Let us make man after our own image, and let him have dominion over the fish of the sea, and the fowls of the air, and the beasts of the earth. From whence it is well inferred, *Non fundatur dominium nisi in imagine DEI.* But yet this seemeth not to com home to our case. For according to this observation, as all men are lords and masters over all inferior creatures, so they should be all fellows one with another, and consequently there would be no rule at all among them; for in a co-equality of power, there can be no predomination, no more then in a consort of musick there can be an harmony where every one sings, or plays the same part. *Nihil æqualitate inæqualius.* Wee must therefore make a further enquiry what regiment or policy was in use first among men. For certain

Gen. i. 26.

it is (however the Prophet spake in his passion), that God did not make men as the fishes of the sea, and as the creeping things that have no ruler over them. It was never intended by his providence, that those noble creatures, whom he had made but a little lower than himself, and under whose feet he had subjected all things, should sink into a confusion among themselves, and trample one upon another.

<small>Hab. i. 14.</small>

<small>Psal. viii.</small>

As to this it may be conjectured upon good grounds, that the first forme of government, after the earth began in any measure to be peopled, was by a single person; it is true, we finde that forme entitled, the rule of paternity and eldership, and it may seem to have had the precedency of monarchy, in that infancy of the world, for about fower hundred seventy five years from the creation, as Syncellus reckoneth it, or according to Pandorus his account, one thousand fifty seven, who calleth that space, Χρονον ἀβασιλοψτεν, the time without Kings. But if we consider the latitude

<small>Salian Annal. Eccles.</small>

<small>Euseb.Fragm. a Scalig.edita.</small>

was

wherewith that paternal and elderly rule was exercised, we shall finde it to have been no other in effect then purely monarchicall; the fathers of nations being reputed as kings in that age, and the eldest of families as subordinate princes under them. That Adam had the dominion over his wife and children, and that he instituted religious rites and ceremonies in his family; as also that Cain had the title of eldership by birth, whereby he was to have ruled over his brother, is generally taken for granted, and is in part literally expressed in Scripture. It may be further observed, that whereas in our Bibles we read, that the sons of GOD saw the daughters of men; the Chaldee, Samaritan, and Arabic translations render it, *Filii principum, filii dominatorum, & filii illustrium,* the sons of princes, of rulers, of nobles; with reference (as the learned Ainsworth is of opinion) to Seth the son of Adam, and the other Patriarchs, who living long, and multiplying to a vast proportion, reteined

<small>Raleigh, l. 1. c. 5.</small>

<small>Gen. vi. 2.</small>

<small>Bibl. Polyglotta.</small>

<small>Ainfw. in loc.</small>

R 4   a foverain

Reineccius.

a soverain power over their respective issues. What that power and authority was, may be collected from the practice of those fathers after the Floud, when for a time that government was resumed: they *Gen.* xiv. 13, 14. & xxi. 24. & xxvi. 31. & xxxviii. 24. took upon them to levy warr, to make peace, to enter into leagues and confederacies, to inflict capital punishments; and wanted nothing but the title and formality of being kings.

And this natural policy (as I may call it) was not only in use amongst those fathers both before and after the deluge, but likewise at one time or other throughout the universal world; so that what power the magistrate had in the state, the father *Aristot. Politic.* l. 1. c. 1. had in the family. Heathen authors are clear in this. Homer saith, that to fathers within their private families, nature hath given a ligislative power, *Natis dat, & conjugibus leges quisque.* Every man was a lawgiver to all that related to him under his own roof, to all that were *Homositioi* (as Charondas

Charondas called them), fellow-trencher-men in his houfe, or (as Epimenides ftileth them) *Homocapnoi,* that lived together within the fmoak of his chimneys. Ariftotle fpeaks home, and in plain terms affirmeth, that a father had Ἄρχτω Βασιλικτο, a regal power over his children; and that *quatenus,* a father, as having a right to command what he had gotten. And in another place, proving out of Homer, that in the beginning people were governed by one king, and the eldeft in the family was king, he maketh the paternal and regal form of government, one and the fame in nature, *Ipfum regnum fuâpte naturâ imperium eft paternum;* and concludeth them to be after a fort convertible, that as the government œconomical, or paternal, was *regnum quoddam;* fo the regal was *quædam œconomia.* And it is not an improbable opinion, that as the chiefeft perfon in every houfhold, was in the nature of a king, fo when many houfholds came to joine themfelvs

Ariftot. Polit. l. 1.

Ariftot. Polit. l. 3. c. 11.

selvs in civil focieties together, kings were the firſt kind of governors among them, *Primum in regum imperio errant civitates, & nunc etiam gentes, ex iis namque qui in regum imperio eſſent, conveniebant,* faith the fame Philofopher; which alfo may be the reafon why the name of father was ſtill reteined amongſt them, who of fathers were made kings: fo Homer, in allufion to this, entitleth Jupiter, the father of gods and men, and king of all. And upon the fame ground they may have feem'd to have kep't up the ancient cuſtome of executing the office of prieſts, which was peculiar to the fathers at firſt. Wee finde both thefe titles concurring in the perfon of Melchizedeck, who, if he were Sem (according to the common opinion), was himfelf one of thofe ancient fathers, and yet king of Salem, and prieſt of the moſt high GOD, *Rex idemque facerdos.* Hereunto I may add what divines have collected out of thofe words unto Reuben,

<small>Vid. Platon. de leg. l. 3.

Ariſtot. Pol. l. 1. c. 1.</small>

thou

Thou art my my first born, &c. the ex-   Gen. xlix. 3.
cellency of dignity and of power: that as
the eldest of the family, he was to have
been by vertue of his birth right, *Primus
in regno & primus in facerdotio,* if by de-
filing his father's bed he had not forfeited
that title.

By what hath been delivered, as to this
particular, wee may understand, that however the frame of government by fathers
and elders may seem to have been set up,
before there was any notice of monarchy
in the world; yet (admitting that) it was
no other in the true and genuine exercise
thereof, then monarchy under a milde and
gentle name; and at last grew up to be the
same in title with it, or was otherwise
swallowed up in it; *Rexque patrem vicit,*   Ovid Metam.
as the Poet said in another sense; that   l. 12.
soverain regiment, like Moses his rod, devouring those weaker rods of paternity
and eldership, and by degrees ingrossing
the dominion of all. For after that by
multi-

multiplication of families, natural affection grew cold, as being derived and drawn further from the spring; and that by separation of families into divers parts and quarters, for convenience of habitation, there grew up distinct interests among them, every one seeking to provide for itself: it came to pass, that obedience (the fruit of natural reverence) being overshadowed with pride, envy, contention, and violence, utterly withered and fell away; whereupon necessity and reason made both the foolish and the wise understand at once, that there was no way to prevent the general confusion of mankind, but by yielding a general obedience to order and government. Then it is said, that to take away competitions and factions, which might arise between persons of equal merit and condition, people were glad (where they had the power) to come to an agreement among themselvs, to make choise of some one in whom they confided, who, bearing the sword of justice,

might

might be a protection to them; and where they had not that power, they were fain to submit to those, who by force and tyranny usurped, and held that authority over them; and this Irenæus giveth to be the reason, why GOD at first appointed kingdoms; because that when men had cast off the fear of the LORD, and were becom wilde and degenerate, and unnaturall to their own kinde and blood; it might be a just punishment upon them, to be put to live under the fear of man, and the restraint of humane laws: whereby, as in mercy, they might be kept from devouring and consuming one another; so, in justice, they might be taught to know the difference between the service of GOD and of man.

Iren. contr. Her. l. v.

But yet for all this, I cannot so easily admit the precedency in time of the œconomicall, or paternal, form of policy, before the regal; because (as I signified at first) I conceive much may be said in maintenance of it, as to the point of antiquity,

quity, more then for any other government. That there were kings in being, long before the floud, and even from the first population of the earth, may appear upon several accounts; not only from a possibility that many princes or dynasts of the Egyptians (mentioned in their records) might have lived in that age, and a probability, that the cruel oppressions in those times might proceed from a rougher frame of rule then the paternal; but also from divers positive testimonies out of history. To pass by what Mela, Pliny, and Solinus witness, that the city of Joppa stood before the deluge, and was not so wash'd away with it, but there remained to after times a memorial of the King and of his brother Phineus engraven in certain altars of stone: Abydenus and Appollodorus (both authors of great name, and often cited by Josephus and Eusebius) give an account of ten kings, that reigned in Chaldea successively in that infant age; of

Bolduc. de Eccles. ante Leg. l. i. c. 15.

Mela, l. iii. Plin. l. v. Solin. c. xlvii.

Euseb. omnimod. Hist. Græc. Fr.

whom

whom Horus is said to have been the first, and Xisuther, or Sisuther, the last; in whose time they say the floud came. And this wee have confirmed, by the authority of the true Berosus, that most ancient and learned priest of Belus, who out of the memorials of the time before the floud (which were saved out of the water at Heliopolis, or Bethshemesh, and after removed to Babylon, and there preserved for posterity) compiled the body of the Chaldean or Babylonian History; a work which, if it were now entirely extant and incorrupt, might justly be reckoned a treasury of antiquity. St. Augustine hath a conjecture, that Cain assumed the state of a king, in his city of Henoch, and that those of his genealogy reckoned in Scripture (which are but six) were such as succeeded in the regency after him. And if that be true, which Philo writeth, that Cain built six cities more, besides Henoch, which he reckoneth particularly by name; as likewise

Euseb. Præparat. l. vii.

Augustin. de Civit. Dei, l xv. c. 20.

that

that, which Berosus hath delivered concerning Henoch, that it held the command of the whole earth, from the rising of the sun unto the going down thereof, that conjecture may seem to be grounded upon a rational probability.

But besides this, wee may argue from proofs and inferences out of story, that the line of Seth was not behind hand with that of Cain in point of honour. Not to mention that suspected letter from Alexander to Aristotle, where it is said to have been written of Kenan, the grandson of Seth, that he reigned as emperour over all the world; the memorial whereof was extant, in certain tables of stone remaining in (I know not what) island in the East Indies. Bolduc hath the confidence to deduce a succession of monarchs, from Enos to Cainan, and so down to Noah. But Cedren, an author of more credit, and instructed out of the ancients, traceth this soverainety further upward, and fixeth it upon Seth,

Selden. Titl. of Honor, p. i. c. 1. §. 3. Ex Joseph. Ben. Gorion, l. ii. c. 11.

Seth, whofe name we meet with in Plutarch, as honoured and revered by the Egyptians, for their moft ancient parent and patron of the firft tradition. Unto which, if wee fubjoyn the affirmation of Conftantine Manaffes, that the Egyptians were the firft people in the world that admitted kingfhip; and add to that, the authority of Eufebius, who accounteth the Egyptian kingdom to have been coeval with the beginning of the world; we may, putting all together, fpell fomthing out of thofe teftimonies in favour of this opinion. But Cedren ftops not at Seth, but lays his axe to the root, and makes Adam himfelf to have been the fole governor or commander of all mankind, fo long as he lived. Somthing in confirmation of this it hath been obferved by Eufebius, that the gods of the heathen, Saturn, Jupiter, Mercury, Vulcan, Apollo, were all kings of their feveral times; and he is not alone in this opinion. Herodotus fpeaking of them, affirmeth, that

Plutarch. de Ifide & Ofiride.

Conft. Man. p. 14.

Eufeb. Demonftrat Evangel. l. iii. c. 9.

Cedren. compend 9.

Eufeb. de Præpar. Evangel.

Euhemerus apud Laƈt.

that they were firſt deify'd by the Egyptians; and Ariſtotle, relating to the monarchical government in that primitive age, calleth it heroic, wherein people made men kings, and then made thoſe kings, gods, according as they had merited of them, either by the invention or tradition of arts and ſciences to them, or by protecting them by their arms and counſels. Now, if we conſider what was ſaid before out of Conſtantine Manaſſes and Euſebius, touching the antiquity of the Egyptian kings, and their date of times (which could not be all feined), and why thoſe forementioned kings were enrolled in heaven by them, we ſhall finde ſom reaſon to ſubſcribe to the conjecture of thoſe learned men, who gueſs Saturn to have been no other than Adam, under whoſe reign they reckon the golden age; in alluſion to the ſtate of innocency, or the ſimplicity of that infant age; and who account Jupiter to have been Cain, the firſt founder of cities, as indeed he was

ant. 1 ii de Fals Rel c. xi. Herodotus in Euterpe Ariſtot. Pol.l.iii.c.10.

of

of Henoch; and Mercury, Apollo, and Vulcan, the inventors of paſtorage, muſick, and ſmithſcraft, to have been Jubal, and Tubal, and Tubal-cain. This laſt in name hath ſom affinity with Vulcan, whoſe ſiſter (and poſſibly wife, according to the cuſtome of that time) was Naamah, whom St. Auguſtin expoundeth to have been Venus. Upon the whole matter, that be droll of Egyptian kings, and gods, taken up afterwards by the Phenicians, Phrygians, Cretans, Greeks, and other nations, may ſeem to have been but the commemoration of ſome of thoſe fathers before the floud (beginning from the firſt man Adam), who reigned over their reſpective deſcendants; and by their piety, juſtice, and fortitude merited that honour from them. But of this ſubject, the moſt learned Selden hath written more at large, in his excellent book of the Titles of Honour, wherein I may ſay, his pen hath done honour to thofe titles, I referr the curious reader to him.

These are ancient things; and the remaining memory of them appeareth unto us no otherwife then like a crack'd mouldred picture, whereof we may difcern here and there fome decayed lineaments and touches, but cannot poffibly make out the full and entire proportion. Neverthelefs, they are not fo totally to be rejected, but that fom veneration may be due to the reliques of thofe times: there may be fomthing pick'd out of thefe fragments, that may ferve to give them a value; as Ochus found reafon to fett an high price upon the afhes and rubbifh of Zidon, after it was demolifh'd. Neither doth it follow, that becaufe the Scripture is filent as to thefe particulars, therefore there fhould be no credit given to any other teftimony: for even in Scripture we meet with feveral paffages relating to the ancient records of the

Diod. Sicul. l. xvi.

the Jews; as thofe frequent references to the books of Jafher, Nathan, Shemaiah, Iddo; to the ftory of Jannes, Jambres, and to the prophecy of Enoch before the floud; none of which were reckoned canonical, or were for many ages before extant, and yet were held of good repute; or otherwife, we may believe, they would not have been cited, and quoted in the word of GOD. And though thofe firft times were branded by Varro and Epiphanius with the marks of ignorance and barbarifm, yet it is not to be doubted but that divers memorials of them did remain to after ages, both by way of tradition and cabala, and alfo by writing. For the firft, it was moft fhort and eafy from Adam to Methufelah, who was contemporary with Adam 243 years; and from Methufelah to Noah, who lived together with that longevall father no lefs than five hundred years; by whom, and his fonns, that knowledge might be conveyed to fucceeding generations.

Jofh. x. 13.
2 Chron. ix. 29, and xii. 15, and xiii. 22.
2 Tim. iii. 8.
Jud. v. 14.

Cenfor. in. de die natal. c. xxi. Epiphan. contra Hær. l. i. c. 1.

nerations. For the other, it may be conceived upon probable grounds, that it was not unknown in that firſt age of the world, and therefore, with much more eaſe and certainty, the memory of things might be continued, through the floud, to thoſe following times. To ſay nothing of that ſtory, in Annius his Beroſus, of Noah his writing, upon a monument of ſtone, the paſſages of his being ſaved in the arke, or of that Hiſtory of the Giants, reported by Cedren to have been written by Cainan, or, as others would have it, by Sala; or of that book of the Creation, ſaid (together with ſom other pieces) to have been written by Adam (all which we paſs by as forgeries and rabbinical fancies). It is a truth undeniable, according to the judgment of St. Auguſtin, that Enoch, the ſeventh from Adam, did write *nonnulla divina*, divers divine things. Of his prophecy St. Jude maketh mention; and of his book of aſtronomy, both Origen and Tertullian,

<small>Kircher. l. i.</small>

<small>Auguſtin de Civit. Dei, l. xv.</small>

<small>Jude. Ep. v. 14.</small>
<small>Origin. Hom. xxviii.</small>

Tertullian; the latter of whom affirmeth, that he had seen and read some pages thereof. Suidas faith, that letters were invented by Seth; which Cedren confirmeth; the proof whereof remained on his pillars, erected and inscribed by him; one of which was said by Josephus to be extant in his time. But Salianus taketh that to be an argument rather of the use of letters in that age, then of his invention of them. Not to speak of that marke, fett upon Cain by the hand of GOD, which some of the ancient Hebrews would imagine to have been one of the letters of Abel's name; most likely it is, that Adam was the first inventor of this admirable knowledge; and that he had it, by revelation from GOD, and taught it to Seth and his posterity. And in this, both the Hebrew Doctors, and the Chaldeans, Arabians, Samaritans, Abassins, and Egyptians do all agree; which being admitted, as upon probable grounds, it is not difficult to conceive,

Tertullian de habit. mulierun.

Genebrard.

Walton in Prolegom ad Bibl. Polyglott.

conceive, that the intelligence of thofe times, before the floud, might by tradition, or writing, be delivered to after ages. So Tertullian guefseth, that the works of Enoch were preferved by Noah in the ark; and Berofus affirmeth (out of the Chaldean records), that the written memorials of thofe times were by a divine command buried in the earth at Heliopolis, and fo kept from being buried in the floud, as we have before mentioned. And this is confirmed by Eufebius, out of Abydenus, who faith, it was Xifuther (the laft Chaldean king) that did this, being forewarned by Saturn of the floud to come. But I proceed.

In the following times, after that univerfal deluge, we may with more eafe, and by a better light, trace the original, the growth, and propagation of monarchy. There are authors, and thofe of great antiquity and credit, as Alexander Polyhiftor, and others, that derive the beginning of it from

Marginal notes:
Tertul. de habit. mulier.
Eufeb. de Præpar. Evangel.
Vid. Bolduc. l. i. c. 1:, and l. ii. c. 6.

from Noah; and that by a title preceding the floud, neer about one hundred and fowerſcore years, and continued through it under the name of Xiſuther, formerly ſpoken of. That Noah held the ſame regard and veneration among the families of his ſons, as Adam did among his after their generations, is very probable, and Cedren averreth it, who writeth of him, that in the nine hundred and thirtieth year of his age, being warned by God, he made his laſt will and teſtament, and thereby divided the earth between his three ſons, allotting unto every one his portion, with command that they ſhould not invade each other. To Sem, he bequeathed the countries of Paleſtina, Perſia, Bactria, and all thoſe eaſtern parts as far as India: Ὅς καὶ τὴν κρεμονιαν διεδέξατε μετ᾽ αυτον, who, as he ſaith, ſucceeded him in the empire. To Cham, he left Egypt, Mauritania, and the reſt of Africk; and to Japhet, all thoſe territories that lay from Media weſtward,

Cedren. Hiſt. comp. f. 12.

as farr as Gades, and the Brittish islands.
Thus far Cedren. But we shall not rest upon his single evidence. Selden is of of opinion, that all those sons of Noah were kings over those respective patrimonies assigned to them by their father. For Sem, if he were the same person with Melchizedek (as most authors agree he was), we have an express testimony in Scripture, that he was king of Salem. As to Cham, it is recorded of him by divers ancient writers, that he was intitled Zoroaster, of that cognomination the first; and that he reigned in Egypt, and was there deifyed by the name of Jupiter Hammon; and of Japhet, Bolduc out of Methodius, giveth this testimony, that he was king of Europe.

But we have a sure word to ascertain us, that shortly after Noah issued out of the arke (som say, little more then seventy years, which was so soon almost as the surface of the earth could be throughly dry), Nimrod,

Marginal notes:
Seld. Titl. of Honor, l. i. c. 1.
Kircher. de orig. Lit. L. i. c. 2.
Bolduc. de Eccles.
Seld. Tit. of Hon. l. c. 1.

Nimrod began to take his pleasure in hunting; who, from that invention (as Cedren affirmeth), was placed among the stars of heaven, and called Orion; and therefore the constellation of the dog was joined with him. But saving that fancy, it is evident, that as Cleopatra advised Anthony to fish, so, without help of any such advice, Nimrod did take the boldness to hunt for provinces and kingdoms; and that was his game. But besides this, there are good proofs to evince, that not only in the following days of Serug, but even in the reign of Nimrod (if not before it), divers others claimed free warren in the world, as well as he. We read of Cush his father, and Misraim his uncle, that they took the same liberty, the one in Chaldea, the other in Egypt; both by order of their father Cham, as Kircharus, out of the ancients, hath observed; and of Chanaan, that he about that time, out of a desire of soverainety, and contrary to the express will

Plut. in Vit. Anton.

Kircher. de' Orig. Lit. l.i.

and

and testament of Noah his grandfather, invaded that part of Palestine, which after took denomination from himself, and by fine force conquered it from Sem his uncle; whereupon it followed, that the children of Israel (who were the lineal descendents from Sem) grounded their title to the land of Canaan, as that unto which God and nature had given them a right. Unto these I might add Assur, the son of Sem, and Javan, the son of Japhet (both contemporaries with Nimrod); the one, king of Ninive, the other king of Greece, which in the prophecy of Daniel is stiled the kingdom of Javan. To say nothing of Arphaxad, Egialus, and others, who in that juncture created themselves kings and emperors also. From that time forward, as Salianus affirmeth, almost every nation sprouted up into a kingdom. Epiphanius is positive in the case, and, without reckoning by almost, accompteth the seventy-two heads of families of the sons of Noah, metioned

Gen. x. xi.
P. Martyr. in Gen. c. 10.

Dan. viii. 21.
Joseph. Antiq. l. i.
Euseb. Chron.
Theoph. ad Autol. l. ii.
Salian. Ann. Eccles.

mentioned after their generations, among their people, according to their tongues, to have been all of them foverain princes, and commanders in chief, over their refpective countries and nations. It were endlefs to deduce particulars: let it fuffice, as to us, that this very ifland of Great Brittaine is particulary fett down by Eufebius, Cedren, the author of the Chronicle of Alexandria, and others, as one of thofe kingdoms which belonged to Gomer and his brethren, the fons of Japhet; the memorial whereof did not only remain amongft the Gauls, who were commonly called Gomeri and Gomorei, as Jofephus and Zonaras affirm; and who, in all probability, were the founders of the Brittifh nation; but is, at this very day alfo, reteined amongft the Cambro Brittains, who are called Cumri, in their own language, with no great variation from the other, as the learned Cambden hath obferved.

_{Eufeb.Chron. l. i. Cedren.l.xiv. Chron. Alexand. p. lxi. Jofeph. Ant. l. i. Polyd. Virg. Hift. l. i.}

_{Cambd. Britann.}

Befides this recommendation of monarchical

narchical government, from the antiquity therof I suppose there may be, not unfitly, som arguments drawn from the principles of nature, to maintain it. There are some among the ancient philosophers, that take the elevation of monarchy from the government of the sun over the planets and other starrs, and from the predomination of the moone over the air, and separated souls. But without the help of a Jacob's Staff, we may observe a character of it in inferior creatures; *Rex unus apibus:* the very bees have their king. Phile describeth his court, his state, his guard, with as much particularity as if he had liv'd in a hive. *Dux unus in gregibe in armentis rector unus.* Flocks of sheep and goats, heards of oxen and deer, have their single leaders, and seem to be conducted by instinct to covet that forme of rule. And upon the account of the same speculation it was, that Seneca made that inference, *Naturæ esse, potioribus deteriora submittere.* How connatural this principle

Herm. Trismeg.

Minut. Octav. Phile de Anim.

Sen. Ep. 90.

principle of government is, in an especial manner to mankind, may appear by the practise of the Indian salvages, who are but a little better then a kind of men beasts. *Homines bestiæ,* or *Homines* (to use Ennius his phrase), men in effigie; and yet are taught, by the meer dictate of common reason, to cast themselves into this political mould: so that hardly in the world any nation can be found so imbrutish'd, but that more or less it reteineth somthing of monarchy in the constitution of it. To come nearer to our own homes, every family hath the image and superscription of Cesar upon it; as it is, *imperium unius*. No servant can serve two masters. Nay, to come home to ourselvs, every man hath at once both a natural family, and a natural kingdom, within his own minde: *Nella Signiora di se,* to use the Italian phrase: his soul commanding his body. *Herili impe-rio,* as a master his servant; and his intellect ruling his passions and affections, *im-perio*

Luke xvi. 14.

Aristot. Pol. l. i. c. 3.

perio civili, & regali; as a king his subjects. So that in reference to a natural principle (if there were no more in it), we may conclude this particular, with the expression of Asinius Gallus to Tiberius, *Unum reipublicæ corpus unius animo regendum.*

Tacit. Annal. l. i.

But to lay aside philologies and fancies, I am the rather inclined on the side of this forme of government, because it is, and from all antiquity hath been, the most agreeable to the complexion and genius of this nation. It is not improbable altogether, but that even from the first plantation of this island after the floud, by the children of Gomer, this policy may have been in use here, both in regard it was then most commonly exercis'd by those heads of families, by whom the nations were divided in the earth, after the dispersion at Babel; and therefore most likely to be continued by their succeeding generarations; and for that in the enumeration of those kingdoms, which apperteined to Gomer,

Gomer, this of Brittain is expresfsly by name, and under that title recited, as we have already intimated out of Epiphanius, Eufebius, and others. Concerning the deduction of it, there hath been, and yet is, much difference of opinion. Nennius the Brittan, or (as in fome copies he is called) Gildas derived it by large fteps (like an Alman leap) from Adam to Noah, from Noah to Brutus, and fo downward by Belinus to Caffibelinus: with whom Thalieffin, furnamed Ben Beirdh, the chiefeft of the bards, and all the Brittifh genealogifts agree, as to the extent of the pedigree, but with this variation, as to the perfon of Brutus, that Nennius will have him to have been the fon of Heficion, or Ifichio, or Hefichio; perhaps Afhkenaz, the firft fon of Gomer, from whom the Hebrews call the Germans, Afhkenazim, avouching for his authority the tradition of the ancient and firft inhabitants of Brittaine: and they affert him to have been the fon

Ex Vetuftiff. M. S. Nenn. fub.tit.Gildæ.

Ar. Montanus in Peleg.

of

of Sylvius Posthumus, the fourth in descent from Æneas, affecting (as the Gauls did) a Trojan original. Geoffry ap Arthur of Monmouth, the author of Polychronicon, Matthew of Westminster, Giraldus, Leland, and many more, are of the last party. Henry of Huntington, although averse, was afterwards, upon the view of an old Chronicle at Beckinsham (in his journey to Rome) converted to the same faith with the rest, as he himself testifyeth in his letter to Warren Harding, and Upton, are such true Trojans, that they take upon them to blazon Brute's coat of arms, to the great honour of heraldry. But leaving that point to be determined in a court of honour: certain it is, that this opinion was so generally received, that Edward the First made it the foundation and ground of his plea to Pope Boniface, in justification of his invasion of Scotland, that the direct and superior dominion of that kingdom had, from all antiquity, even from

Hunt. in lib. de sumitatibus rerum.

Upton de re milit l. ii.

Th. Walsingh. in E. I.

from Brutus his time apperteined to the crown of England.

On the other fide, there are divers writers, both of our own country and of forrain parts, as John of Wheathamftede Abbat of St. Albans, William of Newborough, Cambden, Selden, Polydore, Virgil, Bodin, Buchanan, (*quorum nominibus affurgo*, to ufe Seneca's phrafe, unto whofe authority I put off my hat), who deny this whole Brittifh ftory, not only as fabulous, but as an entire fable; *non vitiofa, fed vitium* (to make ufe of Martial's expreffion in another fenfe) as corrupt, *in totâ fubftantiâ*, and deferving no credit at all: holding that before the coming in of the Romans, the inhabitants of this country were little more then once removed from the falvage, living (as at this day the Indians of the Weft do) in a free natural fimplicity, without any entire rule or combination among them. That they were divided into many little

Senec. l. 8. ep. 65.

Mart. l. 11. Epigr 93.

Strabo, l. iv.

little states and regiments; and those in all likelyhood, Democratical; according to the custome of the Gauls, and of the Northern people of this very island; who were for the most part swayed by popular counsels, as Dion Nicæus, out of the epitome of Xiphiline, expressly affirmeth, that those here whome Cesar calleth kings, and Strabo kinglings, (Reguli) such as were Cassivellanus, and the fower Kings of Kent, were, upon a true accompt, no other then Generals and Commanders elected by the people to manage affairs, in cases of public danger. And lastly, that in those days, there was no king in this our Brittish Israel (properly so stiled), untill the reign of Augustus; in whose time we read of Cunobellinus or Cynobellinus, entitled King of the Brittains by Suetonius, and Dio; and that both he and those Kings that followed him, were not Free Princes, but only *Instrumenta Servitutus*, as Tacitus termeth them, a kinde

Sueton. in Auguft. Dio. Hift. l. 60,

Tacit. in Vitâ Agric.

kinde of things set up, and imposed upon the poor natives, only to hold them in a tame subjection.

For mine own part, I can look upon this contest with a very calm disinteressed aspect, *superciliis quietus*, as Heracleo said, as being of no faction, but (according to Dr. Powel's advice) indifferently ballanced between those easy natur'd people, that are ready to take every thing for currant, that hath the stampe of the Brittish story upon it, *sine ullo judicii negotio*, (as it is said in Gellius) without giving themselvs the trouble to weigh it in the scale of reason: and those that are so hard of belief, that they will receive nothing at all of it: as if they affected the art that Maldonat maketh mention of, *nihil credendi*. I confess it is an hard matter to make any positive judgment, in a case of so great antiquity; wherein (as in a vast prospect), our eye doth but lose itself, and the further we look, the less we see the image of those times,

<small>Plut. de Orac. defect.
D. Powel. Epist. de Hist. Brit. recte intell.

A. Gellius. Noct. Attic. l. i. c. 15.</small>

Job. iv. 16.

times, appearing to us no otherwise, then as that spirit appeared to Eliphaz, in an obscure confused figure, the perfect form whereof we are not able to discern. But yet in that middle way, between a credulity and an infidelity, I think there may be so much evinced out of the whole matter of that story, as may serve to make it appear, that even in those days of old, before the date of the Julian accompt, I mean before the coming in of the Romans, this country was not such a nothing in nature; (*inane naturæ,* as Pliny phraseth it) nor the people such a no people, as som would fancy: but that from all antiquity (so far as the candle of letters or tradition, can give us any light) here hath been a continual regal form of government.

To make this full weight, I crave but the allowance of those few grains which we usually cast into the scales, unto other nations in like case. As first, that in matters of the originals of people, and states,

it

it is fitter (as Myrsilus saith) *credere ipsis gentibus quam remotis,* to receive the testimony of natives, then of forreiners are strangers, as of those that in reason must be more concerned for, and better acquainted with the monuments of their own country, then any others; upon which account we give more credit to Josephus his history of the Antiquities of the Jews, who, was himself a Jew, and well versed in their writings and records, then to what is delivered upon that subject by Diodorus, Strabo, Justin, or Tacitus: who, though otherwise authors of great reputation, yet being aliens, from the Commonwealth of Israel, concerning the truth, erred grossly.. If this right be deny'd to the poor Brittains, their memorial must needs perish with them; for until the latter times, they were so secluded from the knowledge, as well as from the situation of the rest of the world, that neither Grecian nor Roman could, for many ages, tell

Myrsil de Bello. Pelasg. c. 3.

tell whether there were such a people *in rerum naturâ*, or no; and after that Polybius and Lucretius, had discovered their name, it remained a question, Whether the country were an island or a continent; and as Dio ingenuously confesseth, much was said on both sides, by those that knew not what they said, but wrote by conjecture, as their fancy led them; and therefore, in this case, there is no choice, but either the Brittains must be admitted, to clear their own antiquities, or none else can do it.

In the second place, I conceive it no unreasonable demand to have it granted, that in these enquiries, it may be justifiable to admit traditional proofs. This is no more courtesy then is allowed all nations under the cope of Heaven; there being no other evidence possibly to be produced, in cases *de originibus*, before the use of letters, which seldom or never were in practice in the infancy of any governments or states; but then, when they were com

margin: Polyb. Hist. l. 3.

margin: Dio. l. 29.

up towards their full growth, the first knowledge of the first times was deriv'd this way: *Ex animo in animum fine literis, medio intercedente verbo,* as Dionyſius faith. The Grecians that brag'd ſo much of the antiquity of their learning from Cadmus, would not (as Joſephus telleth them) ſhew any one record of that time; but were fain to reſt upon tradition, for proof, that they had been taught to read, and write. And it ſeems, the practice of writing was then ſo rare, that for ſome hundreds of years after Cadmus, there was nothing of that nature extant among them; Homer himſelf, though ſo good a Poet, yet, as it is ſaid, was not ſo good a penman as to write his compoſures, but delivered them by word of mouth in ſeveral canto's or ſongs: and ſo committed them to memory. Livy makes a queſtion, whether the Romans had any thing to ſhew, for all the times before the ſacking of their city, by the Gauls, more then fames, and reports

Joſeph. cont. App. l. 1.

Liv. Dec. 1. l. 6.

paſſed

passed from one hand to another, which Polybius calls Ἀκοτιω ἐξ ἀ.κομȣ : and he affirms directly, that they had not an historian among them untill the second Punick warr, when Fabius Pictor began to write, so that for three hundred years at the least, if not five hundred, they were fain, in a great measure, to make use of that cabinet of air tradition, wherein to lay up the remembrance of their beginnings, and first progresses in the world. All this, notwithstanding we are contented to give credit to Greek and Roman authors, though taking up their knowledge of antiquity, upon the accompt and trust of this kind of Cabala. And why we should not act our historical faith with the same Charity to our own writers, when they are necessitated to use the like freedome, I for my part, see no reason. And this the rather, for the honest care taken by the Brittains, to preserve their memorials uncorrupt, by calling their bards who were
 their

their living chronicles to examination at their Sethua's, or public conventions; and there paſſing their cenſures upon what was commendable or faulty, either in the matter or forme of their poems.

In the laſt place, I take it for granted, that the intermixture of ſome fictions in an hiſtory, though it be extremely blameable, yet is not of ſuch a leavening nature, as to ſowre it ſo, that it ſhould be therefore rejected in the whole lump. Upon thoſe terms, Herodotus, Livy, Dionyſius, Halicarnaſſus, and almoſt all the old writers might bid farewell to the world, if they were queſtioned, and take their journey into the fire. There is nothing more evident, then that the ſtory of Hector, Achilles, and Agamemnon, was poetically written by Homer, with a world of fabulous amplifications; and yet Metrodorus is juſtly derided by Tartianus, for denying that whole ſtory, becauſe ſome particular paſſages in it appeared to be incredible.

Diodorus

Diodorus said well, *In prifcis rebus, veritas non eft ad unguem quærenda.* In matters of antiquity we muft not be so fcrupulous as to meafure the truth of every thing to a nayl. It is not to be denied, but that Geoffry of Monmouth and his followers, have (out of a vain defire to fet off and glorify the Brittifh nation) corrupted the memorials of thofe old times by interlarding them (as for tafte's fake) with divers unconfcionable tales of princeffes errant, and Hobgoblins, and giants (fuch indeed as are only fitt to make men laugh, and children cry), wherein, like the afs in the fable, they have but don hurt where they meant to kiffe; and by endeavouring to make lies fhew like truth, have made truths fhew like lies; and confequently, have leffened the whole ftory by magnifying it. But yet with Livy's, *detur venia*, with a by you leave, I think fomthing may be indulged to them; if together with thofe wild chimeras and fancies, they have brought

Liv. dec. 1. l. 1.

brought any thing of probable truth to our knowledge, which otherwise would have been buried in oblivion; though they have done it but *commodè* (according to Varro's expreſſion). ^{Varr. l 6. de Ling. Lat.}

To this I may add a fit caution, as to the cenſure of that ſtory, which paſſeth under the name of Geoffrey; that there ought to be a diſtinction had between what is of the ancient ſtory that is rational, and what is of his invention, palpably fabulous. For it is delivered from good hands, that the ſtory was never of his compiling; but anciently written in Welch, and communicated to him by one Walter, Archdeacon of Oxford, in the reign of King Stephen; and by him tranſlated into Latine; but moſt falſly and corruptly: ſo that he may be better entitled, Father of the lyes, then Author of the ſtory; and we may be at a liberty to believe the one, and to reject the other. It is true, if the current of time would ever run backward, and

and restore things past to our perfect view and knowledge, it might be a point of judgment for us to suspend our judgment, in expectation of that dooms-day (as I may call it), when the secrets of all antiquity should be revealed. But that being not seperable, I hold it no disgrace, rather to give credit to what hath been anciently delivered by our own writers, then to turn infidel, and believe nothing.

With these preliminary concessions, I think the Brittish history may be admitted as passable, at the least for so much as may serve to prove, in a general way, that a *tempore quo non extat memoria*, we have had a regal form of politie among us, in this island. Polydore himself doth not absolutely deny that; but likeneth the condition of Britaine, as it was of old, to the state of Italy, as it was in his time, wherein there were several sorts of governments, at once co-existent, some under single persons, others administerd by the nobility and

<small>Polyd. Virgil. Hist. l. 2. in proæm.</small>

and people; concluding neverthelefs, that thofe that were ftiled kings here (as Caffivellanus among others), were only fuch as had acquired fomthing a greater intereft then their fellows, in their refpective cities. It feemeth, that Polydore was fo jealous of doing any honour to that poor people, that he was contented, rather to do injury to his own country: for within the compafs of his memory, as there were the republiques of Venice and Genoa flourifhing, fo there was likewife (which he might have taken notice of) a King of Naples, and other foverain princes that look'd upon themfelvs as holding their quality by a better title then the being *potentiores inter alios*, which foundeth little more then the being the beft men in their parifh. As to his expreffion, *aliæ civitates ab uno principe,* &c. (which term he took out of Cefar) it is well obferved by Cambden, that Cefar, by the word *civitas*, doth not denote a particular citie (as we ufe it), for that

Polyd. Virgil. ibid.

that he termeth *oppidum,* a town; but a whole entire people living under the same laws, so that every city was then understood to be a country, as may more plainly appear, in the case of the Trinobants, whom Cesar calleth, *firmissiman earum regionum civitatem,* and saith that Immanuentis reigned over them before Cassivellanus. But out of Tacitus and Ptolemy, it is evident, that they were a people or nation, inhabiting (as Cambden affirmeth) the counties of Essex and Middlesex; and that Londinium was the capital town, in all those parts, both for traffic and provisions. So that according to that account, Immanuentius or Cassivellanus, though but intitled Kings of the Trinobants, were more then mayors of a town; and were not so straightned in their jurisdiction, but that they had land-room enough to swing a scepter in.

 I insist not upon the lineal succession of threescore and eight kings mentioned in the

Cæsar de Bello Gall. L. 5.

Tacit. Annal. l. 14.

the Brittish catalogue, to have reigned here for the space of one thousand and fourty years before the coming in of the Romans. But that some of those princes may have held the government in this island, I hold it not incredible. The particulars delivered concerning Dunwallo, Belinus, and Lud, are such as carry the language of soberness, if not of truth, with them. We yet retein the substance of the Molmucine laws, touching the observation of just weights and measures, the keeping up of tillage, the appointment and priviledge of high ways, (to this day called, the king's high ways). The memory of Belinus and Lud is still extant upon the gates of London; and why the city itself should not own the denomination from Lud, with more probability then either from Cambden's Lhown, which signifieth, a wood or grove; or from Selden's Lhan Dien, the Temple of Diana; or from Verstegan's Lunden, a town in Sconeland; I see no reason, there appearing nothing againſt it, but bare conjectures, and that prejudicate opinion againſt the whole Brittiſh ſtory, that it is not ſo, becauſe it is not ſo; which is a reaſon without reaſon. Dr. Powell, a ſober man, and learned in the Welch antiquities, holdeth, that from the time of Dunwallo Molmucius (which was about five hundred years before the incarnation of our Saviour) the monarchy became divided into ſeveral principalities, every one abſolute within itſelf, and all ſo confederate, and link'd together, as that in any common danger, they were ready to unite under one ſupreme command.

But to lay aſide our own authors, as having poſſibly too much of the party in them: I think it may, with probability enough, be evinced out of the Roman hiſtorians, that the government by kings of greateſt antiquity among us. Tacitus ſeemeth to imply ſo much in the life of Agricola; where, writing of the Britains,
he

he faith, that in old time they were governed by kings *(olim regibus parebant)*; which cannot, with reason, be understood of the time subsequent to the Roman invasion: for there passed but little above one hundred years, between that and the reign of Domitian (wherein he wrote), and during all that while there was a continuance of kings among them, from Theomantius, who succeeded Cassivellanus, unto Arviragus and Marius; and therefore, I conceive, that expression must of necessity have a retroaspect to a time of further antiquity. And if I might have leave to offer my humble conjecture, I should think that the following words of that excellent historian, in the same place *(Nunc per principes factionibus, & studiis trahuntur)* do, without any straining, signify the contradistinction between that form of rule then exercised in the nation, under several princes or kings, (as he elsewhere calleth them): and that which was formerly practised, in the days

Tacit. in Vit. Agris.

Id. Annal. l. xiv.

of old, when the whole island was under one entire government. It is manifest out of Dio, that notwithstanding the invasion made by Julius Cesar, the succession of our kings remained uninterrupted unto the reign of Claudius; during which time this country *Suis Regibus, concessa, & suis Legibus est usa,* as he saith; and so much is acknowledged on all hands, that that intervall was filled up, from the time of Cassivellanus, with the successive reigns of Theomantius (according to the Brittish history) son of Lud, and nephew of Cassivellanus; of Cunobelinus sonne of Theomantius; and Guinderius son of Cunobelinus. That these kings were absolute, and not meerly titular (as some would suggest) may be gathered sufficiently, both from the coines of Cunobelinus, yet extant among us (which shew him, to have carried the badges of soverainety) and likewise from the circumstances of the story of Guinderius, who, so far from recognizing the dominion

Dio. l. liii.

minion of the Romans, that we finde him taking arms againſt them, *ob non redittos transfugas*, as Suetonius writeth; which was a quarrel only incident between free ſtates.

^{Suet. in Claudio.}

But to come out of the dark into a clearer light. Under the following emperors, we meet with an unqueſtionable catalogue of kings; ſome, nobly diſputing the liberty of their country, with them, in deſpight of all their rods and axes: as that brave Caractacus, invincible, though conquered, and triumphant in his chains: others, couching under the power of that vaſt empire, and contenting themſelves to hold their own, though by a beneficiary title. But the laſt ſhall be firſt; the immortally glorious, and happy Lucius, the laſt of Brittiſh, and firſt of Chriſtian kings. It is true, that from him, unto the time of Vortigern, there was a diſcontinuance of this government, by the intercurrent rule of Propretors, and Lieutenants, and Vice-gerents:

gerents: yet upon the declination of the Roman intereſt here, it recovered, and got up again, as Gildas teſtifieth; and notwithſtanding all thoſe great changes, by the coming in of the Saxons, Danes, and Normans, hath ever ſince, untill this horrid eclipſe) enlightened our hemiſphere. As to that objection againſt our monarchy, that it was, of old, broken and divided into ſeveral parcells: I conceive that doth not alter our caſe, for a monarchy is the ſame, as to the forme of politie, in a ſmall, that is in a large dominion; as a ſixpence, or a ſhilling, hath the ſtampe of a king upon it, as well as a twenty ſhilling piece, or the greateſt coyne, and is as currant. Therefore, as Beda ſaid of the Saxon Heptarchy, that it was a monarchy in an heptarchy: ſo, although the Britains were anciently ſo cantonized (as is above mentioned) into ſeveral territories: yet there being no dependency among them, of one upon another, but every one being abſolute within itſelf;

itself: we may say, they were but so many monarchies in little, and every state was a monarchy, as well as if all had been but one. To that opinion of Dio Niceus, that the northern people of this island were governed in a republican way, by popular councils, I think it enough to say, that it is his own opinion, and nobody's else: for I find not one of the ancients concurring with him: and therefore, since he doth not, according to law, *testari de modo scientia*, in avouching his authority, upon which his information is grounded; I shall take the liberty to respit my belief, untill I see a better proof to convince mee. But I have done, and have no more to say (having indeed said too much already) upon this point; but that these forementioned reasons, drawn from the consideration of the laws of the land, the oath of allegiance, the covenant, from antiquity, nature, custome, are inducements to mee, and obligations upon mee, to endevour the restauration

tion and continuance of our monarchical government, and do binde me as a sacrifice with cords to that altar.

I deny not, but there may be other forms of government, in their kinds, and seasons of good use: Aristocracies and democracies are no new things under the sun (but that none are so exact and perfect as the monarchical, may appear by this, that monarchy is the principle whereinto all others are resolved. *Interitus rei arcetur. per reductionem ejus ad principia.*) When the popular state is corrupted into anarchy, the remedy is, to contract the power into the hands of some persons of eminency; which is the generation of an aristocracy: and when those persons fall to divide, and run into factions and emulations, the way to reconcile all, is to unite the power in one supreme command, which is the constitution of a monarchy, and the last and most perfect reduction. And therefore it was prudently advised by Darius, in that great
consultation

consultation, touching the settlement of the state of Persia, that they should do best to fixe upon a monarchy at the first, because after all seditions, and divisions, and changes, they were sure they must come to determine in that at the last. It is true the interests of the populacy and nobility are considerable; but, like som druggs, they work not so well simply taken, as in a mixture; they do best when they are compounded and corrected with a regal power. The Commons and the Lords have their respective operations; but without the influence of a king upon both, there would be nothing but confusions, and exorbitancies. Heraclitus said truly: If the sun were wanting it would be night for all the *Plut. de Fortunâ.*

Notwithstanding all this, I am not so partial to monarchical government as to think it of such a perfect habitude, that nothing can distemper or empaire it. It may grow sowre with too much setling.

As the popular and aristocratical estates are apt to lose themselvs; the one in a turbulent unjust rule of a confused multitude; the other, in a factious usurpation of a few great ones. So the monarchical way degenerate into an arbitrary lawless tyrannie. There is no crown incorruptible but the crown of glory. The time was (as it is said), when this government was in a state of innocency; when vertue created kings, and kings were not better men then others, because they were kings, but were made kings because they were better men then others. *Non poterat potentior esse, nisi melior.* When kings ruled by their example, and having no law, were a living law both to themselvs and others. When love kept people in fear, and the greatest punishment that could befall a subject was to hear his king say, he would be king no more. But those fair days were none of the longest. It hapned to kings (thus elevated above the common sphere of mortality), as it happened

Sen. Ep. 90.

happened to thofe angels that kept not their firft ftation; that being taken and inveigled with the conceit of their own fublimity and glory, *cæcutiebant in fuo fulgore,* they were dazelled with their own luftre; and thereupon forgat their fubordination to GOD, neglected their duty, and fell. They became vain in their imaginations; and as it was faid of Antipheron, that which way foever he look'd he faw his own image before him, *ante fe idolum fui*; in all their undertakings they grew to have their own intereft in their eye; and inftead of governing according to right and equity, they acted as if (according to that bafe expreffion of Anaxarchus unto Alexander) juftice itfelf had not been to direct them to do juftice; but only to fhew that what they did was juftice. From whence it hath com to pafs in many places, that the people, madded with their oppreffions, have caft off their obedience unto them; and breaking all bonds of duty

Ariff. de Memor. et reminife.

Arrian de expedit. Alexand. l. 5.

duty, have offered violence, both to their persons and governments; as we read in the example of the Cyrenians, Argives, Messenians, Arcadians, and others. What should I say more? Certain it is, that there hath been a great declination and falling off in kings and princes, from their primitive integrity.

But it doth not follow from hence, that there is such an original sinn, in their function, as should corrupt all that come after. It is no consequence that all kings must be tyrants; because some tyrants have been kings; nor that regal domination ought to be abrogated, because the exercise thereof hath been abused. If this logique may pass for currant, there is no forme of politie upon earth, but may, upon the same ground of reason, be taken away. I stand not to justify the mal-administration of any government whatsoever: neither do I herein, so much as in a thought, reflect upon the honour of his late Majesty,

whose

whose memory shall remain sacred, and glorious, when the name of his enemies shall rot and stink. But in a general way, I think I may speak it as an inoffensive truth (I am sure I mean it so), that so long as there are governments, there will be misgovernments: wickedness will croud into the place of judgment, and that which is crooked will not be made straight. *Vitia* Tacitus. *erunt donec homines.* That which I aim at, is, the re-establishment of a monarchy circumscribed and entrenched, and as I may say, fortified with good laws: unto which that kind of absolute, illimited, arbitrary rule above mentioned, is diametrically opposite. In plain terms, my heart's desire is to have that government restored again, by King, Lords, and Commons, under which we, and our forefathers for many ages have happily flourished. Of which I never think, without Fulgentius's contemplation of the Heavenly Hierarchy. It was a government for majesty, beauty, and order,

comparable

comparable not only to the best forms that ever were practised; but to the best ideas that ever were fancied. A Democratical Aristocratical monarchy, so excellently well proportion'd, and contemper'd, as it were, *ad pondus*; that the King could not say to the Lords, I have no need of you; nor the Lords to the Commons, we have no need of you; but all were fitly joyned together and compacted by that, which every one supplied, according to the effectual operation and working in the measure of every part. But it is a melancholique thing to remember how happy we were. I wish the sense thereof might lead us to a closure of this schism, which is among us; and to a resettlement of that politie, which, as it is in itself the most noble, and to this nation the most proper and connatural: so it is the sole authority established among us; and that whereunto, both by our allegiance and covenant, we stand most strictly obliged.

I always

I always look'd upon thofe ties that bound mee to the maintenance of monarchy, as likewife knitting my heart, and affections, and endeavors, to the prefervation and defence of his late Majefty, his perfon, crown, and dignity, againft all attempts, and confpiracies whatfoever. And though my engagement may feem to have crofs'd, and interfered with this profeffion, yet I can fafely fpeak it, as in his prefence, who is the Searcher of all hearts, who is my witnefs, and will be my Judge, that in the greateft animofity and heat of the warr, my foul never harboured a thought, to the prejudice of his Majefty's perfon, or the diminution of his juft power and greatnefs, and that I would fooner have perifhed ten thoufand times, then to have touched the lapp of his garment, otherwife, then with honour. All the ends I had in the carrying on of that fervice were but to bring things to a fair and peaceable iffue; that there might have been a general payment

of

of all duties. That God might have had his fear; the King his honour; the Houses of Parliament their priviledges; the people of the kingdome their liberties and proprieties; and nothing might have remained upon the score among us, but that debt which must be ever paying, and ever owing, love.

And therefore I utterly abhor and detest that inhumane, impious proceeding against his late Majesty, as an act (considering all circumstances) not to be parallel'd in any story, since the world began. I look upon it, as *mutum peccatum*, a sinn, not fitt to be mentioned among the Gentiles. If that be true, which some naturalists have observed, that a serpent which hath kill'd a man can never after shelter itself in the earth again: *Quia vox sanguinis clamat, & terra fontis exigit pœnas*, I should think that the earth should refuse to harbour, or to bear those viperous creatures, that, contrary to the faith of both kingdoms,

Marginalia:
1 Pet. ii. 17.
Plin. Nat. Hist. l. 2. c. 63.
Phil. de Animal.

kingdoms, contrary to all example among Proteſtants, and beyond all example of Papiſts, or Heathens, have preſum'd with wicked hands to ſeize upon and impriſon his Royal Perſon, to try him without law, and to execute him without conſcience, as a murtherer before his own door, in the capital city of the kingdome; all this, after he had granted, in the laſt treaty, more then any King ever granted to any Parliament, and more then any Parliament ever demanded of any King; and more then this Parliament, in the beginning thereof, could have thought, or wiſh'd. Certainly the voyce of this blood crieth aloud unto GOD, from the earth, for vengeance; and there cannot but be a ſevere inquiſition for it. It is true, becauſe ſentence is not executed ſpeedily, therefore judgment may ſeem to wink, but it ſleepeth not. I remember, Seneca, in his natural queſtions, diſcourſing of the ſeveral ſorts of thunders, and of their ſignification (according to the

Sen. Nat. Quæſt. l. ii. c. 42.

obſervation

observation of those times) maketh mention of one, which he calleth *Fulmen prærogativum,* a prerogative thunder, with this character of it, that the comminations thereof might be delayed and deferred for a while; but never finally averted. And I am verily persuaded there are some vapors of that kind, even now in gathering, which howsoever they may appear at present, but as a little cloud out of the sea; and the effects thereof may seem, by those interveniencies to be retarded and put off: yet they will never leave working till they have vented themselvs with terror to the destruction of those regicides, and to the confusion of all those that have said, we have no King, what shall a King do unto us?

<small>Hosea x. 3.</small>

Upon the same account, I renounce, and absolutely disavow, whatsoever hath been acted, in order to exclude his Majesty that now is, from this imperial crown, as in itself illegal and null. And according to the tenor

tenor of my allegiance and covenant, I acknowledge his Majesty to be the lawfull King of this realme of England, and of all the kingdoms and dominions annexed thereunto, by a clear and individual right of succession, as next and immediate heir, without reference to any condition or limitation; to any intermission, or to any ceremony or solemnity whatsoever; any pretended act or proclamation in or under the name of the Commons of England, in Parliament assembled, to the contrary notwithstanding. I look upon myself as obliged, beyond the possibility of any humane dispensation, unto the defence of his Majesty's person, honour, and estate, as farr as I am able to serve him; and according to the latitude of my covenant: in recognition and acknowledgment whereof, I call GOD, Angels, and men, to be my witness: and upon the bended knees of my soul, I beseech GOD, to preserve his Majesty, and to establish his throne, and to

_{1 Kings, iii, 9.} give him an hearing heart, as Solomon prayed for, whereby he may be inclined to give a gracious ear to found and wholefom counfails, and be brought to fuch an happy agreement with his faithfull people, in all his kingdoms, as may put an end to thefe miferable diftractions, and make for the fettlement of truth, in the purity thereof and for the prefervation of peace, between thofe feldom quiet neighbours, fovereignety, and libertie: that fo the union may be more ftrict and firm then ever it was before; and like a bone well fett, the ftronger for having been broken.

I look upon the prefent alteration of government, as a treafonable act, and as no way to be fubmitted unto (no not in *licitis & honeftis*), without forfeiture of allegiance, breach of covenant, and the hazard of participating in other men's fins. _{Hofea, viii. 4.} The prophet Hofea hath an expreffion, they have made Princes, and I knew it not: which may imply, that there may be governments,

governments, that are none of God's making (as I may fay), and which he doth not own, or acknowledge: And I am of opinion, this new devifed commonwealth may pafs for one. It carrieth indeed a title of reformation, and in that refpect may gain upon fome men, that love any thing of that name; as the Emperor Caracalla doted upon all perfons whatfoever (though delinquents and malefactors), that had the name of Alexander; but my fancy is not ftrong enough, to work mee to a compliance with it, upon thofe terms. I like a reformation well, and as well as any man: but it muft be fuch an one as may determine in edification, and not in deftruction, as Jonah's prophecy did, touching Ninive, which, as one fays, was fulfilled. *Everfâ Ninive, quæ mala erat; & ædificata bonâ, quæ non erat.* For this, before that I can fubfcribe to it, I muft take time to confider, Firft, whether we were not well enough without it, and if fo, *Quorfum perditio*

<small>Cufpinian. in ejus vitâ.</small>

<small>Auguftin. de Civ. Dei.</small>

ditio hæc? to what purpose are we at this cost? Certainly the world cannot afford us a better contrived government than what we had; and if we should send never so farr for new models of state, I am persuaded we should gain no better return then the Thebans had from Physon, who having been employed by them to make a collection of the laws of the Lacedemonians (out of a civility they had to conform themselvs to their government, then reputed the most exact and perfect), when he came to make his report, instead of delivering that account, as was expected, he only presented them with halters, whipps, and shackles, and the like utensils of justice: and to unriddle the business, plainly told them, that they had as good laws as the Lacedemonians had; and that there was no other odds between them, but that the Lacedemonians excelled them in the maintenance and execution of their laws. Possibly others may go beyond us in the executive

executive part of juſtice, but for the frame itſelf of our government, and for good laws and orders, I am confident no ſtate under heaven can exceed us; and if the defect were only in the mal-adminiſtration, we had laws in force ſufficient to puniſh that defect.

But admitting there were ſome things amiſs in the frame and conſtitution of our government, it may in the next place be conſiderable of what quality they were. For it may fall out in the reformation of a ſtate, as ſomtimes it happeneth in the cutting and poliſhing of a ſtone, that it may be prejudiced and empaired, with too much pointing and forming. *Dum formas minuis;* nay it may be crack'd, and broken, and ſpoiled. And therefore herein ſtatiſts do many times imitate lapidaries, who, if they meet with a flaw, that may be ground forth without prejudice to the ſtone, they will go to work upon it; but if they finde it to be ſuch, as cannot be taken out with-

out abating the ſtone too much, or without hazard of breaking it, they will not meddle with it. They may, upon occaſion reform, and alter things, that ly looſe in a ſtate; ſuch, as like the chaff among the wheat, may, with a little labour, be winnowed out: but what things are ſetled by long cuſtome, and rooted, like tares among the wheat, ſo that they cannot be pluck'd up, without hazarding the good ſeed, they will look upon as *mala bene poſita,* and think better lett alone then changed; when their very eaſineſs to alter and change may bring a greater prejudice to the body of the government, then there can come benefit by the change to any part. Again, it may be thought upon, as to the order of proceeding in this reformation, whether it had not been better to ſettle amendments fair and ſoftly, and by degrees, then in a precipitancy to put all things at once into a confuſion. The way to repair an houſe, is not, with Samſon, to break down at
once

once the pillars that support it. It may be further inquirable, whether it were reformation that drew on this change, or a desire of change, that pretended this reformation. Many, especially where the people are the predominant party, affect nothing but change, *mutationibus ut remediis utuntur:* They think they are as they should be, when they are not as they were. These never settle in a mean, but like ponderous and weighty bodies down a hill, they run away with themselvs, and stop not where they should, but when they go no further.

But taking it for granted, that the former frame of state was faulty, not only as in reference to the decay of some outhouses, or in the inferior offices, but in the very fountion; that the leprosy were so spred, and had so fretted in all parts of it, that neither scraping, nor new plaistering, could serve the turn, and that there could be no way to repair it, but by pulling all down; and that there were no other motive to it, nor

Levit. xiv.

end

end in it, but to sett up a better building in the place. It may be demanded, first, whether it had not been prudential, to have agreed upon a new model, before we had destroy'd the old fabrick? The Jews had a law, forbidding them to demolish an old synagogue (though it were to re-edify another) before they had built up a new one to supply its place. I wish others had been as wise in their generation. But next, and lastly, it may be the question (supposing this business must be done), who are fitt to be the surveyors of the work, and who are authorized to doe it? According to reason, no authority can justify the making of this formal and essential alteration in the government; but that, which first constituted it, and gave it being; which, whether it were vested in the body of the people, that is, in *toto populo*, or in the major part thereof, or in some selected persons, as representees of the rest; or in the nobility, as the most eminent, and of greatest

Ainsw. in Levitic. xxvi. 31.

greateft intereft in the kingdome, it cannot be certainly determined. But in which foever of thefe it were (as in fome of thefe it muft be), moft certain it is, that the gentlemen fitting at Weftminfter had no title to this authority, who could neither be faid to be the people, nor any confiderable part thereof; nor their reprefentative, nor the nobility, I am fure: but were only a ninth or tenth part of an Houfe of Commons, which is a half part of a Parliament, thirty or fourty perfons, feldom more (and for the moft part, not fo many); who fitting under an armed power, and thereby, according to their own ordinance of the the 20th of Auguft 1647, being difabled from acting any thing as an houfe; prefumed neverthelefs (upon the advantage of that force) to imprifon, feclude, and drive away all the reft of their fellow members; to vote down the Houfe of Lords; to affume the full power of the Parliament; to cut off the King; to attaint his iffue;

and

and to change the whole frame of the government, into a confusion called a Commonwealth; whether this be a reformation; or whether these people, so qualified, had authority to reform, let GOD and the world judge. For my part, till I see more need of a reformation (as to the whole body of the government), then I can yet apprehend, I shall willingly dispense with this; and till these gentlemen can shew a better commission for what they have done, then I have yet seen, or can understand, I shall look upon their authority as a meer usurpation and tyranny; upon their votes and orders as null and void; and upon all they have acted, as treason in the highest degree: and I cannot submitt to them, cannot in my conscience, without violating obligations, from which no earthly power can give me a discharge; and therefore I do still adhere to the preservation of monarchy in these dominions, according to our laws and fundamental constitutions;
and

and unto the maintenance thereof I shall willingly sacrifice my life and fortunes. I was borne under a monarchy; and I desire to dy under it, and (rather then fail) with it.

For the constancy of my affection to the service of the Parliament, I may say (if it were my last breath) with that good Theodosius, *Dilexi*. I wish I had been capable to give a better demonstration of it, then I have don by my poor services; which I shall presume to justify no further, then they have been faithfull. Possibly I might have made more brick, if I had had more straw; but with that allowance of force that was assigned to mee, I may speak it without vanity, I was not *Servus piger*. I have been in several perills, both among enemies and false brethren: in wearinefs and painfulness, and watchings often. If at any time I miscarried in my attempt (as who may not ? the dice being no where so uncertain as in the field), it was *operosa infælicitas*

infælicitas unto mee: I ſtrained myſelf in miſſing my aim, and my failing was my puniſhment. I would be clearly underſtood: I am not ſuch a ſtranger to my duty as to aſſume any thing of merit in all this: if I had done more, it was no more then I ought to have done: if I have don leſs, I ſhould have thought it *nihilo minus*. I was ſo wedded to the Parliament intereſt, and paſſionately deſirous to advance it, that I may ſay with Martial, it was a diſſatisfaction to mee, that I did no more then I could do: *Si tantum ea præſtabam, quæ poſſem.* What I was, I am; and by that marke I would be known. My affection to the Parliament (that is the Publique) was no morning dew: though the ſun hath look'd upon mee, and ſcorched mee to a degree of blackneſs; though I have ſuffered many ways in my eſtate, in my liberty, in my reputation; yet nothing hath been of force to exhale that. They write of Creon, in the tragedie, that he hug'd his beloved daughter

Martial, in Epiſt. ante Epigr. l. xii.

daughter in his armes, in the midft of the fire, and would not quit his hold; but when he could not help her, willingly perifhed with her. I have embraced the Parliament caufe, in the hotteft flames of the warr; and by the grace of GOD, fo long as I can retein my foul within my teeth, I will never defert it; and if I can do it no further, I fhall contentedly mingle my afhes with it. And now, *Oremus:* It may feem a piece of popery to pray for the departed Houfes: but let it be taken how it will, I cannot but pour out my foul to GOD for them, That he would be pleafed to look upon them with a merciful afpect, as upon the corpfes of the two flain witneffes, caft out and defpifed; and to breath himfelf into them, and revive them, and fett them up again in his good time: that being quickened, and acted by his fpirit, they may, according to their firft profeffions, fettle what is amifs, both in the church and civil ftate, and fo re-eftablifh the throne of his Majefty

Majesty, that the world may bear witness to their loyalty. In that way, I doubt not, but GOD will be with them, to uphold and maintain their proceedings: so that in the midst of all trepidations and fears, when the foundations reel and stagger us, we may with boldness write upon their doors (as the good people of Antioch wrote upon theirs, in a great earthquake), CHRISTUS *vobiscum, state.*

As to the union between the kingdoms, I may affirm, as in the presence of heaven, that according to the tenor of my covenant, I have constantly desired, and endevoured, the preservation thereof; and I am still clear in it. Indivision is the *primum bonum,* the felicity of the glorious Trinity, the Heaven in Heaven. And this union (with the blessing of Almighty God) must be the means to establish the felicity of these kingdoms, as to their earthly and temporal condition. So much I am for it, that in my private thoughts, I could wish the

wood

wood of Judah, and the wood of Joseph, England and Scotland, both concorporated and substantiated together, in one tree, that they might be no more several people, nor distinct kingdoms. However, it is the prayer of my soul, that in amity and brotherly conjunction, they may be but one called two, or (according to that character of Proærefius and Hepheſtion) two, and one, eternally and inseparably united. Those Milo's, that affect to shew their strength in renting this tree, may they come to be caught like him, in their own device. Let them be divided in Jacob, that would divide Jacob, and make a schism in the Israel of GOD.

Eunapius.

Valer. Max. l. ix. c. 12. Pausan. in Eliac.

Thus have I, according to my weak talent, or mite, or what you will call it, given an accompt of my stewardship, as farr as it hath had reference to these troubleous times. I have done it justly, and without setting down fifty, 'or fowerscore for an hundred; and without blanching any particularity,

ticularity, that I thought malice itself could not object against mee. I have likewise unbosomed myself, and endevour'd to urn my inside out, and to shew, that my actions and intentions, my words and deeds have been *unâ forma percussa,* of one and the same stamp; and that I have rowed no other way then I have look'd. I am not ignorant of the hazard I run in this, rather to provoke malice, then to satisfy reason; and possibly I may have the same fortune that Praxiteles had, who seeing his face represented in a glass with some disadvantage, would needs break the glass in pieces, but then every piece yeelded him the same prospect, and he did but multiply that unpleasing reflection. My impatience to see myself misrepresented, may but increase animosities and clamours, and railing accusations against me. *Qui replicat, multiplicat.*

But I have cast the die, and chosen rather to run that hazard, then not to discharge

<small>Sen. l. 1. Ep. 34.</small>

charge my conscience by offering up this oblation to truth. The worst that can befall mee, shall be nos. to me. For that matter, the world and I are upon an even score: it never yet deceived me, because I never yet gave it trust. I thank GOD, I can despise the worst. I have weighed poverty, and banishment, and imprisonment, and death; and I have found them light in the balance. I know how to want, and have to abound. I can be at home, abroad, and a free man in prison *(Omnis probus, liber.)* I can finde life in death. If the cruelty of man take all I have from me, I can say with Paulinus, *Domine, ubi sunt mea omnia, tu scis.* There is an house, not made with hands, which they can never sequester. If I be put to seek my bread again, with my poor family, I can comfort myself, as that father did, with the consideration, that the earth is the LORD's, and the fulness thereof. He that feeds the ravens, and clothes the lillies, will provide

1 Pet. i. 4.

Heb. xi. 16.

food

food and raiment. I have a better country then this, that is, an heavenly, unto which the way is alike every where.

If I be continued in prison, it shall not trouble mee. I have lived in prison, ever since I was born: my body is no other to mee but *aliud ergastulum,* a prison, and a worse prison then that wherein I lye. I am both a prison, and a prisoner to myself. The world is but a common goal. *Magis carcer, quam ipse carcer.* A prison, wherein those, that have greatest power and authority have greatest bonds upon them, and are greater prisoners, then those whom they imprison. *Magis vincti, quam ii qui ab eisdem vinciunter.* In the straitest confinement that can be putt upon mee, it is the refreshing of my soul, that I can walk with GOD, and have my conversation in heaven. I may be shut up; but GOD cannot be shutt out. *Etiam & hic Deus.* He is my keeper; and, therefore, though in prison, I can defie a prison. *In carcere etiam*

Philostrat. in Vit. Apollon. l. vii. c. 12.

etiam carceri renuncio. But mine enemies will take away my life! Return unto thy rest, O my soul. The worst which they can do, is but that which is best of all. *Profunt nocendo.* They may kill mee, but they cannot hurt me, as P. Thrafeas Pœtus said of Nero. If I fall, I shall fall, as some have fancied the Antipodes to do, *furfum*; I shall fall upwards into heaven. O death, where is thy sting? O grave, where is thy victory?

But I have done; and let the issue be what it will, I shall humbly acquiesce in the good Providence of GOD, and take that portion contentedly and thankfully, which he shall think fitt to carve unto me: without being so unmannerly, as to reach over my neighbour's trencher, for a better bitt. His blessed will be done with me, and in my submission and obedience to his will, *Fiat voluntas mea.* If I shall finde favour in the eyes of the LORD, he will reintegrate mee in my former condition, and in the

Pfal. cxvi. 7.

Phil. i. 23.

Xiphil. in Nerone.

Epictet. Enchir.

2 Sam. xv. 26.

comforts

comforts I enjoyed with it. But if he thus say, I have no delight in thee; behold, here am I, let him do to me as seemeth good unto him.

FINIS.

A

ÆLIAN quoted, 138
Ælius, his strange inclination to anger, 134
Æmilius Probus quoted, 158
Agitators, who, 112—address letters to the Generals Cromwell and Skippon, 114—their complaints, 118—and demands, 119—apply to Skippon to represent the state of their grievances to Parliament, 122—demand a reparation for the commitment of Ensign Nicholls, 123
Agreement declared in 1647, how violated, 33
Ainsworth quoted, 247, 314
Aldermen of London, their defection, 188
Alexander, allusion taken from his empty chair, 136
Alphonso, his wish, 28
Anaxarchus, his observation to Alexander, 299
Androcydes, why so careful in painting fish, 216
Antigonus, his remark on the strictly-guarded Eumenes, 158
Antipheron, remark concerning him, 299
Antipodes, how supposed to fall, 325
Apollinaris much employed in apologising for the Christians, 2
Apollonius, his tacit oratory, 189
Aquinas alluded to, 145
Aristarchus described by Dionysius, 11
Aristides much employed in apologising for the Christians, 2
Aristotle, his rule for enemies, 8—his distinction between a good citizen and a good man, 14—quoted, 98—his doctrine of lies, 212—quoted, 247, 248, 250, 271, 299
Army, what they effected, 29—their standing proportion, 42—their representations considered by the Parliament, 65—importune the King to stay with them, 157—their bold requisitions to the Parliament, 159—enjoin the Houses to raise no more forces, 164—present a daring and bitter remonstrance to Parliament for the suspension of the eleven members, 167—impute to them the sin of Aaron and of Ham, *ib.*—present still stronger manifestoes, 170—withdraw towards Salisbury, 172—compared to Jehu, 173—called upon to bring proofs against the members, 174—compared to Benhadad, 178—and to the soldiers of Vitellius, *ib.*—compared to sea mills, 179—the House moved against them by the eleven members, 180
Arrian quoted, 299
Atelepiades, his opinion of distempers, 31
Athenæus quoted, 153
Athenodorus, his mode of forming a judgement of diseases, 29
Augustine, Saint, alluded to, 232, 254, 262
Austin, Saint, alluded to, 204

Bacon,

INDEX.

B

Bacon, Lord, quoted, 75
Battin, Vice-admiral, holds a council of war respecting the departing members, 202
Beggar, his jewel, 23
Benedict, Pope, the Ninth, hazards which he ran, 99
Bennet, Moses, employed to publish the dangerous army petition to Colonel Butler's regiment, 72—avows to Captain Molineaux that he undertook the business with the consent of the General, 73
Bernard, Saint, alluded to, 204
Berosus quoted, 264
Birch, Colonel, presides at the Committee for distributing pecuniary relief to the officers and soldiers, 133
Bodin quoted, 275
Bolduc quoted, 254, 264, 266
Boy, his remark on striking his mother-in-law, 179
Boys, allusion to them and the frogs, 204
Bracton quoted, 242
British history, inquiries concerning it, 273 & seq.
Buchanan quoted, 275

C

Camden quoted, 269, 275, 288
Cæsar quoted, 288
Caracalla, his strange predilection in favour of all who bore the name of Alexander, 309
Cassander quoted, 231
Cedren quoted, 34, 257, 262, 265
Charles the First, alarming consequences of his demanding the five members, 27—quoted, ib.—his arguments in the case of ship money, 37—the oblation at the feast of the army, 119—seized upon at Holdenby, 135—used like the empty chair of Alexander, 136—informed the Houses, through Lord Dunfermlin, of the design against him, 137—importuned by the army to stay with them, 157—averse from complying, ib.—strong expression of his determination to resist, were any one to stop him from going to the Parliament, 158—continually watched by the army, ib.—inclines a little to the solicitations of Cromwell and Ireton, ib.
Charondas quoted, 249
Christians, orthodox, how contributors with the Novatian faction, 228
Christians, primitive, false accusations advanced against them, 2
Cicero quoted, 3, 172, 189
City commissioners, their seducing representation of the temper of the army, 161
Cleopatra, her advice to Anthony, 267

Clotworthy,

INDEX.

Clotworthy, Sir John, employed in settling the manner of drawing out the forces for Ireland, 42, 44—acquaints the General with the contents of a dangerous petition, 51—presents copies of a petition to the House, 59—deputed to treat with the General concerning the service in Ireland, 77—sends a message to Waller, 105—departs with Waller, 201—receives the thanks of the House, 223—impeached, ib.

Coccianus, how advised by Otho, 4

Committee at Derby House empowered to treat for the affairs of Ireland, 61—and to employ forces on this occasion, 69—send a deputation to Saffron Walden, to treat with the General and officers concerning the service in Ireland, 77

Committee of Safety instituted, 187

Common Council of London, their defection, 188

Constantine Manasses quoted, 257

Corcyra, ridiculous liberty enjoyed by its inhabitants, 29

Cordus, Cremutius, his observation, 5

Creon, the excess of his affection for his daughter, 3:8

Cresinus produces the spells with which he bewitched the grounds of his neighbours, 94

Crœsus, allusion to his son, 25

Cromwell, Lieutenant-general, his regiment put on the new establishment, 66—receives letters from the agitators, 114—sent by the Parliament to the head quarters at Saffron Walden to allay disturbances, 115—why not applied to by the agitators to present the state of their grievances to Parliament, 122—plots the seizure of the King at Holdenby, 136—makes an extraordinary distinction, 145—the King not inattentive to his solicitations, 158—called upon to concur in a clause for the security of the peerage, 193—demurs, ib.—then accedes, 194

Cuspianus quoted, 309

D

Dacres, Lord, deputed to treat with the General concerning the service in Ireland, 77

Deilius, his appellation, 12

De-la-Ware, Lord, appointed to superintend the disbanding of the army, 128—sent by the Parliament as a commissioner to soften the army into obedience, 142

Democritus, his opinion of atoms, 34

Denbigh, Earl of, withdraws from Parliament, 191

Dio quoted, 276, 280, 292

Diodorus Siculus quoted, 261

Dion Nicæus quoted, 276, 295

Dionysius, his description of Aristarchus, 11—quoted, 281

Dormer, Captain, frustrates the attempt of Ensign Nicholls to lead away the soldiers, 93

Dunch, Mr., presents money to Waller, 209

Dunfermlin,

INDEX.

Dunfermlin, Earl of, informs the Houses of the design to seize the King, 138

E

Ecclesiastical history quoted, 237
England, state of, how differing within a short period, 29
Ennius quoted, 271
Epictetus quoted, 9, 325
Epimenides quoted, 249
Epiphanius quoted, 261, 268
Erasmus quoted, 29
Esculapius, for what deified, 26
Essex, Earl of, Reasons for the fomentation of differences between him and Waller, 16
Eunapius quoted, 121
Eunomus, comparison drawn from his grashopper, 59
Eusebius quoted, 232, 246, 254, 255, 257, 258, 264, 268, 269
Evelin, Sir John, withdraws from Parliament, 191

F

Fairfax, Sir Thomas, proportions observed in the levies of his army, 48
Fear, the extraordinary one of being safe, 162
Ferson quoted, 197
Fincher, Quarter Master General, why reproached by Colonel Rich, 51
Fines, Mr. Nathaniel, draws up the engagement for the Lords to stand or fall with the whole army, 192
Fleetwood, Colonel, sent by the Parliament to the head quarters at Saffron Walden, to allay disturbances, 115
Folly and Malice, their imputations compared to the hissing of snakes and geese, 21
Fowke, Alderman, repairs to the army as a commissioner from the city, 150
Fox quoted, 233
Friar John, government of his college, 148
Fulgentius, his idea of the heavenly hierarchy, 301
Fulmen prerogativum, what, 306

G

Gallus Asinius, his expression to Tiberius, 272
Gauls, Celtic, their vain opposition, 201
Gellius, Aulus, quoted, 277
Genebrard quoted, 263

Genera

INDEX.

General, the, (Sir Thomas Fairfax) sends a letter to the Speaker, concerning the dangerous army-petitions, 70—directs Lieutenant General Hammond, Colonel Hammond, Colonel Lilburne, Lieutenant Colonel Pride, and Lieutenant Colonel Grimes to attend the pleasure of the Parliament, 71.—refuses to publish a declaration of his dislike to the proceedings of a part of the army, 80—but promises to interpose, 81—draws up a letter to them, 85—returns to London against the desire of the Committee, 91—A Major of foot kicked in his presence, for professing an inclination for the service in Ireland, 96—returns, as desired by the Parliament, to Saffron Walden, 125—calls a council of war, 129—moves his head quarters to St. Edmund's Bury, *ib.*—informs the Houses that the army had voted down their resolutions, *ib.*—disclaims the design of seizing the King, 138—his strong summons to the city, 145—draws with his army still nearer to London, 154—receives an order from the Parliament to deliver the King into the hands of commissioners, 156—promises the Parliament to call a council of war on the subject of removing the army to the distance required from London, 166—called upon to bring proofs against the Members, 174—the eleven Members move the House against him, 180—his infantry disproportioned to the city forces, 189—engages to stand or fall with the whole army, 192

Geoffry of Monmouth quoted, 274

Gerard, Sir Gilbert, appointed to superintend the disbanding of the army, 128

German peasant, his shrewd remark concerning a Lord, 146

Gibbs, Alderman, repairs to the army as a commissioner from the city, 150

Gildas quoted, 273

Giraldus quoted, 274

Gladiators, Roman, comparison between them and Waller, 18

Gloucester, city of, presents plate to Waller, 209

Gonsalvo, nature of the oath which he exacted from Ferdinand, King of Spain, 197

Goodwin, Mr., presides at the committee for distributing pecuniary relief to the officers and soldiers, 133

Graves, Colonel, thought of to bring the King up to London, 137

Greave, Colonel, his regiment put on the new establishment, 66

Grimes, Lieutenant Colonel, directed by the General to attend the pleasure of the Parliament, 71——subscriptions ordered to be returned to him, 72

Grimstone, Mr., appointed to superintend the disbanding of the army, 128

H

Hammond, Colonel, called to the bar of the House to answer for having promoted a dangerous petition, 64——his regiment ordered to march up to the head quarters, 71—directed by the General to attend

INDEX.

attend the pleasure of the Parliament, 71—subscriptions ordered to be returned to him, 72

Hammond, Lieutenant General, countenances a dangerous petition, 51—called to the bar of the House to answer for having promoted it, 64—directed by the General to attend the pleasure of the Parliament, 71—subscriptions ordered to be returned to him, 72

Harley, Colonel, avows the petition of several regiments of the army 57

Henry of Huntingdon quoted, 274

Heracleo quoted, 277

Heraclitus describes a particular style, 190

Herbert, Colonel, his regiment ordered to march up to the head quarters, 71

Hercules, how using his sword, 70

Hereford, city of, presents plate to Waller, 209

Hermes Trismegistus quoted, 270

Herodotus quoted, 257, 258

Hesilrigg, Sir Arthur, appointed President of a Council of War, 15—withdraws from Parliament, 191—called upon to concur in a clause for the security of the peerage, 193—appears to dissent, ib.—then complies, 194

Higden quoted, 274

Holdingby receives a copy of the dangerous army petition, 72

Hollis, Mr., pacifies a tumult of soldiers, 100—advised with by Waller, 105—departs with Waller, 201

Homer quoted, 248, 249, 250

Huntingdon, Major, takes the command of Lieutenant General Cromwell's regiment, 66—proves what crowns and sceptres were promised to the King, 120

I.

Janus, observation concerning him, 226

Jesus Christ, how traduced, 1

Independent party, their offers to Waller, 13

Innocence liable to misfortune, when unprotected, 1

Insurgents break into the House of Commons, and perpetrate much violence, 183, 184—compared to those dreamt of by one in Galateo, ib.—dispersed by the sheriffs and their assistants, ib.

Josephus quoted, 241, 268, 269

Joyce, Cornet, employed to seize upon the King, 136—declares that he received his orders from Lieutenant General Cromwell, ib.

Irenæus quoted, 253

Ireton, Commissary General, countenances a dangerous petition, 51—denies its existence, 58—confuted by a letter to Colonel Rossiter, ib.—gives the House his reasons why no vigorous course should be taken to suppress the petition, 59—his motives for urging to have the evidence against the petitioning officers produced, 76—compared to the people pressing for holy water, ib.—sent by the Parliament

INDEX.

ment to the head quarters at Saffron Walden to allay disturbances, 115—plots the seizure of the King at Holdenby, 136—the King not inattentive to his solicitations, 158—puzzled to advance a charge against the eleven Members, 174—called upon to concur in a clause for the security of the peerage, 193—accedes, *ib.*
Italian, his observation on his horse cutting, 19—his remark, 107
Justinian quoted, 242
Justin, Martyr, much employed in apologising for the Christians, 2

K

Kempson, Colonel, commands some companies ordered to Ireland, 91
King, the. See Charles the First
Kitchner quoted, 262, 266
Knightley appointed to superintend the disbanding of the army, 128

L

Lacedemonian, allusion to him and his oyster, 40
Lactantius quoted, 258
Lambert, Colonel, proposes questions to the Earl of Warwick, 83—represents himself as authorised to draw up a state of all the grievances of the army, 116—his proceedings protested against by one hundred and sixty-seven officers, 117
Leland quoted, 274
Lenthal, Mr., withdraws from Parliament, 191
Lewes, town of, presents money to Waller, 209
Lewis, Sir William, sends a message to Waller, 105
Licinius Proculus, his crime of *fidelity* pardoned by Vitellius, 22
Lilburne, John, his opinion of the employment in the West, 18—countenances a dangerous petition, 51—called to the bar of the House to answer for having promoted it, 64—directed by the General to attend the pleasure of the Parliament, 71—subscriptions ordered to be returned to him, 72—proves what crowns and sceptres were promised to the King, 120
Livy quoted, 164
Long, Mr. Walter, departs with Waller, 201
Lucan quoted, 66
Luther alluded to, 204
Lysander, his justice, 37

M

Major of foot kicked in the presence of the General, for having professed an inclination to serve in Ireland, 96
Maldonat quoted, 244

INDEX.

Malice and folly, their imputations compared to the hissings of snakes and geese, 21

Manchester, Earl of, meets the Lords at Hatfield, 191

Mapes, Walter, his description of the Church of Rome, 23

Martial quoted, 8, 31, 77, 197, 275, 318

Massey, Major-general, goes to Ireland as Lieutenant General of the Horse, 68—deputed to treat with the General concerning the service in Ireland, 77—chosen to command in Ireland, 83—calumniated and vindicated, 84

Master of the Rolls called upon by Waller as his vindicator, 99

Matthew of Westminster quoted, 274

Members, alarming consequences of the demand of the five, by the King, 27—the eleven obtain leave to absent themselves for six months, 171—they enter upon their vindication, 177—they move the House against Sir Thomas Fairfax and the army, 180

Merchants present toys to Waller's wife, 209

Militia, ordinance for it reversed, 182—new ordinance for it drawn up and passed, ib.

Milo, to whom his fate is wished, 321

Misery, what the most miserable result of it, 155

Molineaux, Captain, receives the avowal of Moses Bennet, 73

Mornay quoted, 233

Musæus quoted, 153

Myrsilus quoted, 279

N

Narcissus, the master of his master, 173

Nature, her procedure in certain exigencies, 185

Nauclerus quoted, 233

Needham, Colonel, appointed to the command of several united regiments, 66

Nennius quoted, 273

Nicephorus quoted, 232

Nicholls, Ensign, attempts to draw off the soldiers under Colonel Kempson from the service in Ireland, 91—is prevented by Captain Dormer, 92—is sent up to London, and committed by a special order of the House, 93—reparation demanded for his commitment, 123—discharged, 128

Nile, effects of its high rising, 135

Northumberland, Earl of, withdraws from Parliament, 191

Nottingham, Earl of, sent by the Parliament as a commissioner to soften the army into obedience, 142

Novatian faction, how contributors with the orthodox Christians, 228

O

Officers, propositions which they make previously to their answer touching a declaration for Ireland, 47—dissent of others against a dangerous

INDEX.

dangerous petition, 55—these thanked by the House, 61—the treatment at the bar of the House of those who petitioned, 74—their behaviour at their return to the army, 75

Origen quoted, 262

Otho, his advice to Coccianus, 4

Ovid quoted, 9, 32, 217, 251

P

Pætus, his observation as to the power of Nero, 325

Pambo, his lesson, 4—Nova Reperta, 113

Panormit quoted, 33

Parallel lines, how similar to the diversity of opinion and conduct in upright characters, 10

Parliament strongly reprobate the dangerous army petition, 67—consider the representations of the army, 65—vote for uniting particular troops into one regiment, 66—for putting the cavalry of the army on a new establishment, ib.—resolve what regiments shall be employed on the service of Ireland, 67—vote the quantum of their pay, 68—send Skippon, Cromwell, Ireton, and Fleetwood, to the head quarters at Saffron Walden, to allay tumults, 115—vote for the disbanding of all the forces of the kingdom not subscribing for the service of Ireland, 124—pass the act of indemnity, and proceed to votes respecting the army and others, 125—appoint commissioners to assist in the disbanding of the army, 128—recall Skippon, 130—comply with the desire of the soldiers, 131—how, 131, 132, 137—erase from their Journals their declaration against the petition from a part of the army, 133—how requited, 134—resemble Balaam, 141—send new commissioners to soften the army into obedience, 142—order the army to approach no nearer to London than forty miles, 145—stand on their guard against them, 149—greatly perplexed concerning the apprehended demands of the army, 156—send Sir Thomas Widrington and Colonel White to discover their designs, ib.—send an order to require the General to deliver the King into the hands of commissioners, ib.—bold requisition made to them by the army, 159—enjoined by the army to raise no more forces, 164—their fall compared to that of the lion in Theocritus, 190

Parrhasius deceives Zeuxis, 177

Pausanias quoted, 321

Peleûs, comparison drawn from his daughters, 32

Pelham, Mr., called to the woolsack during the absence of members, 185

People, such as know not how to say *no*, 164

Petition, one dangerous, represented as coming from the soldiers, 51—its contents, 52—strongly reprobated by the Parliament, 61

Philo quoted, 270

Philostratus quoted, 189, 325

Physon, his insulting conduct to the Thebans, 310

Pierrepoint,

INDEX.

Pierrepoint, Mr., withdraws from Parliament, 191
Pittacus grinds the Mytylenians, 30
Plain dealing the jewel of the beggar, 23
Plato less a friend than truth, 19—quoted, 250
Pliny quoted, 94, 177, 221, 254, 278, 305
Plutarch quoted, 30, 41, 49, 84, 95, 164, 179, 204, 216, 257, 267, 277, 297
Polybius quoted, 280, 282
Polyhistor, Alexander, quoted, 264
Pomponius Mela quoted, 226, 254
Poole, town of, presents plate to Waller, 209
Pory, Mr., sent by the Parliament as a commissioner to soften the army into obedience, 142
Potts, Sir John, appointed to superintend the disbanding of the army, 128
Powell, Dr., quoted, 277, 290
Praxiteles, his inclination on seeing his face in a glass, 322
Pride, Lieutenant-colonel, countenances a dangerous petition, 51—called to the bar of the House to answer for having promoted it, 64—directed by the General to attend the pleasure of the Parliament, 71
Prinne, Mr., speaks in vindication of the imprisoned members, 222
Proæresius's inseparable from Hephesion, 321
Proximus, his remark concerning Valentinian, 168
Putredo lucens described, 10
Pythagoras, his opinion of the harmony of the spheres, 34—how stiling himself, 98

Q

Quadratus much employed in apologising for the Christians, 2

R

Rabelais alluded to, 148
Rainsborough, Colonel, exception with respect to his regiment, 74
Reineccius quoted, 247
Rich, Colonel, reproaches Quarter-master-general Fincher, 51
Rossiter, Colonel, a letter to him serves for a detection of Ireton, 59—his regiment put on the new establishment, 66—proposed to guard the King with his regiment, 157

S

Sabellicus quoted, 28
Saint John, Mr., withdraws from Parliament, 191
Saints, false, described, 11

INDEX.

Salian quoted, 246, 268
Salisbury, Earl of, withdraws from Parliament, 191
Saloway, Mr., employed in settling the manner of drawing out the forces for Ireland, 42, 44
Salvianus quoted, 197
Say, Lord, withdraws from Parliament, 191
Scawen, Mr., sent by the Parliament as a commissioner to soften the army into obedience, 142
Scotch, their great bravery, 216
Scotus alluded to, 145
Scripture quotations, 1, 2, 3, 7, 9, 14, 18, 19, 20, 23, 24, 27, 28, 32, 34, 37, 38, 39, 43, 49, 73, 82, 97, 106, 107, 113, 134, 141, 143, 173, 175, 178, 198, 200, 204, 207, 211, 217, 221, 224, 225, 227, 228, 229, 230, 236, 245, 246, 247, 248, 251, 261, 262, 268, 271, 278, 304, 306, 308, 313, 314, 323, 325
Scroope, Colonel, sent to the Commons with the charges against the eleven members, 176
Selden quoted, 256, 259, 266, 267, 275
Seneca quoted, 13, 21, 32, 134, 165, 173, 204, 270, 275, 298, 305, 322
Silanus, his case, 5
Sin, manner of the first essays and progress of it, 73
Sirach, son of, his expression for duplicity, 7
Skippon, Major-general and Field-marshal, appointed to the command of the forces for Ireland, 68—obtains the remanding of the regiment of Sir Hardress Waller from Newcastle, 71—receives letters from the agitators, 114—sent by the Parliament to the head quarters at Saffron Walden to allay disturbances, 115—yields to the impetuosity of Lambert, 118—declares his intention to go for Ireland, 121—applied to by the agitators to present the state of their grievances to Parliament, 122—he complies, 123—recalled by the Parliament, 130—advises an acquiescence to the desire of the soldiers, 131—sent by the Parliament as a commissioner to soften the army into obedience, 142
Socrates, less a friend than truth, 19
Soldier, heinous crime of detaining from him his pay, 23
Soldiers stop the money sent by Parliament for disbanding the troops, 130—their desires granted, 131
Solinus quoted, 254
Speaker, the, called upon by Waller as his vindicator, 99
Stapleton, Sir Philip, pacifies a tumult of soldiers, 100
Strabo quoted, 59
Suetonius Paulinus, his crime of fidelity pardoned by Vitellius, 22
Syracides, his advice, 4

INDEX.

T

Tacitus quoted, 5, 49, 178, 220, 272, 276, 288, 291, 301
Tertullian much employed in apologising for the Christians, 2
——— quoted, 262, 264
Thearidas boasts of the temper of his sword, 84
Theo, his use of a trumpeter, 219
Theocritus quoted, 190
Trenchard, John, his account of money paid to Waller, 17
Truth, more a friend than either Plato or Socrates, 19
Twistleton, Major, takes the command of Colonel Rossiter's regiment, 66

U

Ulysses madly inclined to return to the den of the Cyclops, 185
Upton quoted, 274

V

Valerius Maximus quoted, 321
Vane, Sir Henry, the younger, sent by the Parliament as a Commissioner to soften the army into obedience, 142
Varro quoted, 261, 285
Virgil quoted, 37
Virgil Polydore quoted, 269, 275, 286, 287
Vitellius willing to pardon the crime of *fidelity* in Suetonius Paulinus and Licinius Proculus, 22

W

Waller, Sir Hardress, his regiment remanded from Newcastle, 71—employed to vindicate those officers who were deemed averse from supporting the peerage, 196
Waller, Sir William, what considerations are palliatives for his sufferings, 3--strong motives for his vindication, 3, 4—confused but not acknowledged reports against him, 5, 6—clears himself from the charge of apostacy, 6—the inclinations upon which he grounded his conduct in the House of Commons, 8—uses the false saints as Moses did his rod, 11—not quitting but deserted by his friends, 13—offers made to him by the independent party, 13—his answer, 14—his reasons for appointing a council of war, 15—continued in his military command, in the view of opposition to the Earl of Essex, 16—receives money from Trenchard, 17—compared to Joash, 18—sent to the relief of Taunton with an inferior army, *ib.*—compares himself to the Roman gladiators, 18—proof of his

having

INDEX.

having acted conscientiously, 19—defends himself against the accusation of endeavouring to break the army, violate the Parliament, and embroil the kingdom in a new war, 20—questions for which he voted, 22—breaks out against the crying sin of detaining the pay of soldiers, 23—criminates only part of the army, 38—applauds the rest, *ib.*—words in which he takes his leave of the army, 40—vindicates himself from the charge of having endeavoured to destroy it, *ib.*—if perishing, will perish like the ermine, 44—acquaints the General with the contents of a dangerous petition, 51—makes a report respecting it to the House, 56—criminates Commissary General Ireton, 57—enabled by a letter to Colonel Rossiter to detect his falsities, 58—his informations concerning the army petition referred to a special committee, 60—animadverts on the letter of the General respecting the dangerous army petitions, 72—compares the petitioning officers to the woman apprehended in adultery, 75—and Ireton to people pressing for holy water, 76—deputed to treat with the General and officers concerning the service in Ireland, 77—result of his deputation, 78, 88, 90, 93—vindicates General Massey, 84—exculpates himself from the charge of being accessary to assaults by soldiers, apprentices, and others, 97, 100, 103—calls upon the Speaker and the Master of the Rolls as his compurgators, 99—pacifies a tumult of soldiers, 100—receives messages from Sir William Lewis and Sir John Clotworthy, 105—advises with Mr. Hollis, *ib.*—defends himself against the accusation of being an incendiary, 107—accounts for his obedience and subserviency to the Parliament, 111—his remark on the bold proposition of the army for the termination of the Parliament, 160—investigates others, 161—his fine remark upon the refusal to hear just petitions, *ib.*—accused again, 163—compares any thought within him of returning to the House to the madness of Ulysses, 185—obtains a pass from the General to retire into the country, 186—being summoned, attends the House, *ib.*—describes the secession of several eminent Members, and the subsequent fall of Parliament, 190, 191, *et seq.*—vindicates himself from the charge of flying from the kingdom, and taking away great sums of money, 200—describes the departure of himself and associates, 201—clears himself from the charge of conveying money out of the kingdom in butter barrels, 205, 210—magnitude of his losses during the troubles of the State, 207—receives presents from different quarters, 209—refutes the false reports against him, 211—vindicates himself from the charge of taking a commission in the royal service, 213—waits upon the Queen of Bohemia, *ib.*—exculpates himself from the accusation of being concerned in the revolt of the ships, 215—and of having interested himself in the Scottish engagement, 216—proud of being an Englishman, 218—compares himself to the Christians in the skins of beasts, 220—refutes the charge of having defrauded the State, 220—defends his vote that the propositions of the King should be taken into consideration, 221—receives the thanks of the House, 223—impeached, *ib.*—imprisoned, 224—expatiates concerning his religion, principles, politics, affections, opinions,

and

INDEX.

and views, 225, *et seq.*—argues in favour of monarchy, 241, *et seq.* —his inquiries concerning the British history, 273, *et seq.*—panegyrises Charles the First, 301—his attachment to him, 303—his detestation of his execution, 304, *et seq.*—his motives for engaging in the civil wars, 303—his solemn declaration in favour of monarchy, 308—his constancy to the Parliament, 317—compares himself to Theodosius, *ib.*—prays for the Parliament, 320—expression of his wishes for an union between the two kingdoms, *ib.*— compares the world to a prison, 324—how, in his own person, enabled to bear imprisonment, *ib.*—may fall like the Antipodes, 325

Walsingham, Thomas, quoted, 274

Walter, Archdeacon of Oxford, alluded to, 284

Walton quoted, 263

" Warning for all the Counties of England," a violent pamphlet, 79

Warwick, Earl of, deputed to treat with the General concerning the service in Ireland, 77—addresses himself to the officers at Saffron Walden, 83—answers the questions from Colonel Lambert, *ib.*— informed of soldiers serving against the Parliament, 121—appointed to superintend the disbanding of the army, 128—remains useless at Chelmsford, 130

Whaley, Colonel, his regiment put on the new establishment, 66

Wharton, Lord, employed in settling the manner of drawing out the forces for Ireland, 42, 44—informs the General of the contents of a dangerous petition, 51—withdraws from Parliament, 191

Wheathamstede, John of, quoted, 275

White, Colonel, sent by the Parliament to discover the design of the army, 156

Widdrington, Sir Thomas, employed in the same manner, 156

William of Newborough quoted, 275

Willoughby, Lord, of Parham, called to the woolsack during the absence of members, 185

Woman, old, her remark on the Mitylenians being ground by Pittacus, 30

X

Xiphilinus quoted, 325

Z

Zenocles, result of his decision with Euripides, 8
Zeuxis deceived by Parrhasius, 177
Zonaras quoted, 269

THE END.

www.ingramcontent.com/pod-product-compliance
Lightning Source LLC
Chambersburg PA
CBHW020326240426
43673CB00039B/929